ETHICAL FOUNDATION OF HOTEL & HOSPITALITY MANAGEMENT

ETHICAL FOUNDATION
OF
HOTEL & HOSPITALITY MANAGEMENT

Edited by
Shambhu Dayal

AKANSHA PUBLISHING HOUSE
NEW DELHI - 110 002 (INDIA)

AKANSHA PUBLISHING HOUSE
4649/21-B, Ansari Road
Daryaganj, New Delhi - 110 002
Phones: 23263193, 9811582579
E-mail: ektabooks@yahoo.com

Ethical Foundation of Hotel & Hospitality Management

First Published, 2006

ISBN 81-8370-070-5

PRINTED IN INDIA

Published by M.P. Misra for Akansha Publishing House, New Delhi - 110 059 and Printed at Tarun Offset Printers, Delhi

Contents

Preface

> Without the help of others, any one of us would die, naked and starved. Consider the bread upon our tables, the clothes upon our backs, the luxuries that make life pleasant; how many men worked in sunlit fields, in dark mines, in the fierce heat of modern metal, and among the looms and wheels of countless factories, in order to create them for our use and enjoyment.
>
> —*Alfred E. Smith*

As is universally regarded, business ethics is a normative discipline, whereby particular ethical standards are assumed and then applied. Professional ethics covers the myriad of practical ethical problems and phenomena which arise out of specific functional areas of companies or in relation to recognized business professions. Hotel and hospitality management is an interesting field of contemporary research and development. The present volume encompasses a field of study with the purpose of preparing people with the expertise, commitment, and skills morally and ethically ready for management, marketing, and operations positions in the expanding hotel and hospitality industry. Definitely, hotel and hospitality management draws upon a wide range of basic disciplines to provide the fundamental knowledge and skills that are required to fulfill the diverse demands placed upon individuals in management positions within the hospitality industry.

We intend here to develop hotel and hospitality management capability through inter and multidisciplinary subject exposure and management applications based on corporate business ethics and social responsibility.

The core of this work includes the following topicsIntroduction; Code of Ethics for Board Members of CIE Group; International Association of Hospitality Advisors (IAHA): Code of Conduct; Workplace: Problem of Ethics and Discrimination; Hotel Ethics Management; Case Studies on Application of Ethics; Issues of Hospitality Ethics; Hotel and Hospitality Industry and Facilities Management (FM); and Guidelines and Concerns in Quality Management etc.

Amply supported by original documents, this book imparts sufficient information about the hotel and hospitality management, ethics management courses. This will help prepare students for management career in the hotel and hospitality service. Hospitality ethics in hotels, motels, restaurants, food service units, casinos, clubs, resorts, fast food franchises, meeting points, conference and convention centers, airlines, tour operators, and travel agencies are given elaborate treatment. Simultaneoulsy, it tends to cover the aforementioned subject areas in their broadest possible terms. A veritable mine of information, this book is unique in terms of coverage, usefulness and perspective formation.

Since the book is substaintially based on secondary sources of information, we owe a deep sense of gratitude to great scholars—academics as well as professionals—on whose works this is devised and developed. As such no claim of originality. Finally, we are grateful to our publishers for materializing our efforts in the present shape.

—S.D.

1

Introduction

> Circumstances are the rulers of the weak; they are but the instruments of the wise.
>
> —*Samuel Lover*

Hotel and Hospitality Management: Role of Ethics

Although most businesses prefer not to articulate their codes of ethics, owners adhere to their own ethical standards. Those who play free and loose promising one thing and delivering a completely different product have a short reign in the marketplace. Most hotels and restaurants have some type of unwritten code of ethics \which mysteriously remain in the heads of general managers. This writer believes that a Code of Conduct articulating the ethics of a hotel chain and/ or restaurant is as important as a sound marketing plan or fine menu.

A code of conduct is meant to encapsulate an organisation's beliefs ad values, which must be internalised and used as a guide in all training sessions., given to all new employees, and explained in detail. It is in fact part of the corporate culture. It must become the mantra of conducting business. Today, more than ever, people pay attention to corporate governance, and propriety of behaviour. Promises must be fulfilled; both product quality and price must correspond to those advertised. A hotel promising ocean-view rooms ands failing to deliver has acted unethically. Similarly, a restaurant menu promising wild Atlantic troll-caught salmon must deliver exactly that and not "farm-raised" salmon that has a completely inferior taste and texture, and which costs much less than the former. In a single location hotel and/or restaurant, the beliefs, values, and principles of the owner automatically get transmitted to actions. When the leader nurtures organisational values, his/her successors are most likely to sustain them for many years to come. When a hotel or restaurant chain expands its operation to internationally, local talent must be hired and trained with regard to: integrity, responsibility, unity, understanding, and excellence. Some Far Eastern companies adhere to the notion of not to creating a monopoly or even trying to acquire a dominant market position. Few, if any, western enterprises would even consider such a code of ethics. Equality of all employees with regard to human rights issues must be dealt with fairly, quickly and equitably to the satisfaction of all concerned. The Code of Ethics once articulated and agreed upon by the owner and/or board of directors must be made available to all employees, Seminars to department hands must be held to disseminate the contents of the document by a cascading process regionally, countrywide, and internationally.

Likewise, a competent, responsible employee in each outlet must administer the code. There is a need to articulate ethical practices and there can be no sound management if they are not vigorously exercised. Serving others is a noble profession and can be practised in a dignified fashion with sound ethical principles to reap the benefits of growth and prosperity.

Developing Patterns

The following model is based on the practices used by Strike and Soltis (1985) in their text titled *The Ethics of Teaching*. These authors developed realistic case studies centered around ethical issues and way of ethical decision making for instructors and administrators in educational institutions.

First, Strike and Soltis evaluated two major types of ethical theories: consequentialism and nonconsequentialism.

The former theoretical perspective is based on whether the consequences of the decision maker's actions were moral or immoral. In short, a consequentialist asserts that the morality or immorality of an action is determined by the consequences of the ethical decision. The nonconsequentialist believes morality or the immorality of an action is determined by sense of duty, obligation, and universal and impartial adherence to principles.

However, the current model expands on Strike and Soltis' model by incorporation of ethical theories of egoism, benevolence, principle into the context of consequentialism and nonconsequentialism. For the purpose of this proposed model egoism aligns with consequentialism and benevolence and principle align with nonconsequentialism. Second, vignettes must be developed based on current and pressing ethical dilemmas as extracted from the organisational setting. This phase allows the learner an opportunity to absorb and identify with the issue as applied to the learner's operational setting. However, it would be a good practice to utilize focus groups to validate a vignette's content prior to incorporating the issue into a vignette.

The purpose of the focus group is to ensure that the issue has relevance to the setting and to management. Third, the "learner" is challenged to read and review the key points of the vignette. Basically, the learner is challenged to reflect upon on "what" (i.e. the issue) is going on in the vignette. Here the learner enters the situation with their own "experiential baggage."

Furthermore, it is the presence of pre-existing internalized values and beliefs (e.g. baggage) that strongly impact the learner's reliance on a preferred ethical precept. Fourth, the learner is challenged to analyze the issue from each theoretical perspective.

This process is intended to raise the learner's level of understanding of the unique differences between the theoretical approaches. This, of course, requires an extreme amount of facilitation by the trainer/instructor because it challenges the learner to adopt an ethical stance that varies from their own personal value system. This stage is also quite complex because it not only analyzes the theoretical perspective, but includes an analysis of how the referent sources (i.e. personal values, immediate work setting, and societal values) interact to influence an individual's ethical decision.

The last step in the proposed model is to compare and contrast the theoretical approaches available to the learner. This process provides an overview and synthesis of the key concepts germane to each theoretical perspective. It is the latter stage of the model that is expected to offer the learner a deeper appreciation of how their ethical conduct is directly linked to organisational effectiveness. Hence, the learning process displayed provides an overview of introducing the learner to an ethical dilemma, the awareness of the issue by conceptualizing through a chosen ethical precept in combination with the immediate influencing referent source, a consideration of the consequences (e.g. trial), application of the ethical decision, and then an evaluation of the consequences.

Also, this model indicates that a feedback loop is part of the process. This feedback loop allows the decision maker the opportunity to make the necessary adjustments in "how" they might resolve a similar situation if the occasion arises again. Still, a caveat to this proposed process of ethical training is that the proper application of ethical theory must be reviewed by a content expert in ethical theory.

More specifically, this "expert" can assist in the development and validation of ethical responses based on the ethical derivatives of consequentialism and nonconsequentialism. In actual practice ethical decision making proceeds through the typical decision- making steps of awareness, information search, alternative evaluation, application and evaluation. In the first step of the model the individual becomes aware that a problem exists. Next, information is sought that aids the individual in conceptualizing and in coping with the problem. In this stage of decision making the individual considers various resolution strategies. Third, the individual adopts one strategy in an attempt to resolve the ethical dilemma. Fourth, the individual applies the selected ethical strategy to the ethical dilemma.

The last step of the ethical decision-making model involves the individual (ethical decision maker) in a monitoring process. Here the decision maker weighs the positive and negative outcomes of the imposed strategy in an effort to adjust the principles to match the situation better. Of course, the type of adjustment taken is contingent on whether a consequentialist or a nonconsequentialist approach is taken.

Ethics in the Hospitality Industry

According to Longenecker (1985), management affects an organisation's ethical performance by the establishment of priorities that direct the ethical conduct of the organisation. He also asserts that the "management process", and particularly the setting of organisational priorities, affects the attainment of ethical performance by identifying those values which seem important to management.

In order to satisfy these duties lodging management must deliver services that meet the needs and wants of its guests. However, during the provision of daily services, management is often confronted with a variety of ethical situations that can leave a lasting either positive or negative impression with the guest, staff, and other members of management. Undoubtedly the image that these constituent bodies collectively hold is directly related to organisational success as directed by management.

The belief that an organisation's ethical climate is strongly influenced by management's ethical conduct has generated a body of academic research that has focused on determining the type and nature of ethical issues that are present in lodging organisations. In general, hospitality researchers have determined that management is confronted with ethical issues surrounding guest rights, empowerment, sexual harassment, equal opportunity, departmental relations, vendor relationships, yield management, community and public relations, and the balance of personal and organisational values (Enghagen and Hott, 1992; Hall, 1993; Hall and Enghagen, 1991; Kwansa and Farrar, 1991; O'Halloran, 1991).

Overall, these studies have reflected on profiling ethical situations and in understanding management's role in resolving particular ethical situations within a service based setting.

2

Code of Ethics for Board Members of CIE Group

> Nature never hurries: atom by atom, little by little, she achieves her work. The lesson one learns in fishing, yachting, or planting, is the manners of Nature; patience with the delays of wind and sun, delays of the seasons, bad weather, excess or lack of water.
>
> —*Ralph Waldo Emerson*

I

General Policy

It is the policy of the CIE Group to maintain its high reputation for ethical behaviour and fair dealing in the conduct of its business.

In many cases decisions as to what is ethical or fair are clear cut and will be obvious to any reasonable person. In some situations, however, there may be circumstances where an element of doubt or ambiguity arises. To help in those circumstances and to protect and guide individual Board Members and Directors of the CIE Group, it is necessary to have a written Code of Business Ethics.

It is not possible to provide for every situation in the Code of Business Ethics. If there is doubt about the probity of any particular situation, the Chairman must be consulted about that situation by the individual concerned.

Objectives of the Code of Business Ethics

The objectives of the Code of Business Ethics are:

(a) to offer guidance to CIE Group Board Members and directors in their business conduct,
(b) to establish an agreed set of ethical principles,
(c) the promotion and maintenance of confidence and trust in the CIE Group; and
(d) the development and acceptance of ethical practices by the CIE Group.

The Code of Business Ethics applies to all Board Members and directors of the Group.

Principles of the Code of Business Ethics

The guiding principles of the Code of Business Ethics can be summarised under seven headings:

— Integrity,
— Confidentiality of Information,
— Legality,
— Disclosure of interest,
— Loyalty,
— Fairness and
— Consideration for Work/External Environment

Integrity

Each Board Member and directors of the CIE Group is expected to observe the highest standards of honesty and integrity in all his/her business dealings.

To this end, as a Board Member or directors, one must:

— commit to compete vigorously and energetically but also ethically and honestly,
— ensure that purchasing activities of goods/services are conducted in accordance with best business

practice and in accordance with the Group's procurement policy,

- ensure that the Group's accounts/reports accurately reflect its business performance and are not misleading or designed to be misleading,
- refuse bribes, gifts, hospitality, benefits or offers of preferential treatment which may affect one's ability to make independent judgement, and report any such approaches in writing to the Chairman,
- avoid misrepresenting one's position or being ambiguous or misleading,
- reject any business practice which might reasonably be deemed to be improper,
- avoid the use of the Group's resources or time for personal gain, for the benefit of persons/organisations unconnected with the Group or its activities or for the benefit of competitors,
- commit not to acquire information or business secrets by improper means,
- not abuse travel facilities or other privileges and
- whilst acting in his/her capacity as a Board Member of CIE, not act in a manner which could bring the reputation of CIE into disrepute.

Confidentiality of Information

The Group is not yet obliged to disclose information under the Freedom of Information Act, 1997. Any requests for information pursuant to the Act from third parties (including the Department of Transport) must be referred to the Group Secretary or the company secretaries of any of the subsidiaries who will, in turn, pass the request to the Group Secretary. Board Members and directors of the Group should also be mindful of the Group's obligations under the Data Protection Act, 1988 and any requests for or regarding information held by the Group which is subject to the provisions of that Act should also be referred, in the first instance, to the Group Secretary.

Board Members and directors of the Group must, however, support the provision of access by the Group to general information relating to the Group's activities in a way that is open and that enhances its accountability to the general public. In an effort to put this into effect, the Group publishes information on its activities and performance on its web site which is regularly updated.

Every Board Member and director of the Group owes a duty of confidentiality to the Group in respect of sensitive information held by the Group. Sensitive information would include , for example, :

— any information relating to the CIE Group which is not public information,
— commercially sensitive/business information (including information relating to business policies or practices),
— any information relating to the CIE Group which is designated by it to be confidential,
— personal information and
— information received in confidence by the CIE Group.

Board Members and directors are required to ensure that any sensitive information which they obtain by reason of their Board membership or directorship is not disclosed and/or mis-used, whether by competitors of the CIE Group or otherwise. In order to protect such information, Board Members and directors are required to:

— ensure that such information is properly safeguarded,
— exercise due care in communicating such information,
— avoid using such information for personal gain and
— observe appropriate prior consultation procedures with third parties where, exceptionally, CIE is obliged

by law or any regulatory authority, or otherwise, in the public interest, to disclose sensitive information.

Board Members and directors are reminded that the Transport (Re-Organisation of Coras Iompair Eireann) Act, 1986, includes a specific duty not to disclose confidential information unless authorised by the Board or the relevant company or by some person authorised in that behalf by the Board or the company. Confidential information is defined in the Act as that which is expressed to be confidential either as regards particular information or as regards information of a practical class or description. Breach of this statutory duty is an offence which attracts a fine on summary conviction.

Legality

In order to ensure through one's business dealings compliance by CIE with all applicable Government Guidelines, Irish and EU legislation, Board Members and directors are required, to the extent that it is within their power, to:

- fulfill all regulatory and supervisory obligations imposed on CIE,
- comply with the provisions of the Transport Acts, the Ethics in Public Office Act and the Companies Acts which are relevant to them as directors
- co-operate with relevant regulatory and supervisory bodies,
- avoid false, inaccurate or mis-leading entries in records
- ensure that taxation and welfare legislation is upheld by the CIE Group,
- ensure that the Group CIE does not engage in "offensive" tax avoidance transactions (meaning transactions involving uses of the tax code for a purpose other than for which it is intended by the State (including an unintended use of a tax incentive) with a view to reducing the amount of tax to be paid

by the CIE Group or a party to a transaction in which the CIE Group participates),

— ensure one's actions comply with relevant contractual obligations,
— encourage effective and fair competition at all times,
— ensure that the Group's purchasing and tendering procedures and prescribed levels of authority for sanctioning any relevant expenditure are complied with,
— avoid engaging in any illegal or criminal activities,
— comply with controls to prevent fraud including adequate controls to ensure compliance with prescribed procedures in relation to claiming expenses for business travel,
— comply with procedures relating to:
  (a) post resignation / retirement from Board membership / directorship and
  (b) appointment and/or consultancy of Board Members and directors by the private sector, in order to avoid the acceptance of positions following Board membership / directorship which could give rise to the potential for conflicts of interest and to confidentiality concerns and
— comply with the CIE Group's policy on discrimination, harassment, sexual harassment and bullying.

Board Members and directors should use their reasonable endeavours to attend all Board meetings and where appropriate, committee meetings.

Disclosure of Interests

Board Members and directors are required to comply with the provisions relating to disclosure of interests by directors set out in the Transport Acts, the Companies Acts, the Ethics in Public Office Act, the disclosure requirements set out to the Code of Practice for the Governance of State

Bodies, the procedures relating to disclosure of interests established by the Board and the procedures set out in this Code.

Board Members and directors are required to disclose to the Group/Company Secretary details of outside employment/ business interests or interests of any of their family members which are or may be in conflict or in potential conflict with businesses of the CIE Group.

Where a conflict of interest situation could arise for a Board Member or director, he/she must desist from dealing with the contract or situation giving rise to the conflict or potential conflict of interest and may not attempt in any way to influence decisions on the matter.

Loyalty

Board Members and directors must:

— cknowledge the responsibility to be loyal to the CIE Group and fully committed in all its business activities while mindful that the organisation itself must at all times take into account the interests of its shareholder and

— acknowledge the duty of all to conform to highest standards of business ethics.

Fairness

Board Members and directors must:

— comply and ensure compliance by the CIE Group with employment equality and equal status legislation,

— commit and ensure that the CIE Group commits to fairness in all business dealings and

— value customers and passengers and treat all customers and passengers equally and encourage all CIE Group employees to do likewise.

Consideration for Work/External Environment

Board Members and directors must:

- — ensure that CIE Group employees place highest priority on promoting and preserving their own health and safety as well as that of fellow employees, customers and other third parties with whom they come in contact in the course of their employment,
- — ensure that community concerns are fully considered and
- — minimise any detrimental impact of CIE Group operations on the environment.

Responsibility

This Code of Business Ethics which incorporates the policy on disclosure of interests has been circulated to all Board Members and directors who must retain, acknowledge receipt of and confirm their understanding of same.

Review

This Code of Business Ethics will be reviewed at least every two years.

Guidelines regarding Gifts or Hospitality

Board Members and directors should, in their capacity as Board Members / directors, subject to the procedures outlined below, avoid the giving or receiving of corporate gifts, hospitality, preferential treatment or benefits which might affect or appear to affect the ability of the donor or the recipient to make an independent judgement on business transactions.

Gifts

Board Members / directors may accept corporate gifts from suppliers to or contractors who have worked for the CIE Group, provided:

- the gift is one of very small intrinsic value (e.g. diary, calendar, bottle of wine/spirits etc.),
- the gift is unsolicited,
- the value of such gifts accepted in a year from any one source does not exceed Euro 120 and
- gifts with a value exceeding Euro 65 are disclosed to the CIE Board in the case of the CIE Chairman, to the CIE Chairman in the case of Board Members, or the Chairman of the relevant subsidiary board in the case of directors.

In all other cases, the gift should be returned to the sender, with a note advising that acceptance would be contrary to Group policy. Details of returned gifts must be notified at once to the Chairman.

Hospitality

Modest hospitality (including sporting events and golf outings) may be accepted by Board Members / directors in their capacity as such, provided:

- he frequency and scale of hospitality is not more than the CIE Group might be expected to give in return,
- the number of CIE Group staff, Board Members or directors availing of the hospitality is kept to a minimum and
- invitations do not include the provision of travel or overnight accommodation and availing of the hospitality does not identify the CIE Group in a public way with any particular supplier or contractor. Details of hospitality offered in this context, that has been turned down, must be notified at once to the Chairman.

When any Board Member/director (or group of Board Members/directors) of CIE considers that circumstances have arisen where it would be inappropriate for him/her/them to consult CIE's professional advisers and he/she/they consider that, in the furtherance of his/her/their duties, there is a need for independent professional advice, in such cases, Board Members and/or directors should follow the relevant procedures which have been circulated to them or which are available from the Group Company Secretary.

II

CODE OF ETHICS OF CIE GROUP

General Policy

It is the policy of the CIE Group to maintain its high reputation for ethical behaviour and fair dealing in the conduct of its business.

In many cases decisions as to what is ethical or fair are clear cut and will be obvious to any reasonable person. In some situations, however, there may be circumstances where an element of doubt or ambiguity arises. To help in those circumstances and to protect and guide individual employees of the CIE Group, it is necessary to have a written code of ethics.

It is not possible to provide for every situation in the code of ethics. If there is doubt about the probity of any particular situation, the Head of Group Procurement must be consulted about that situation by the individual concerned.

Purpose of the Code of Ethics

The purpose of the Code of Ethics is to offer guidance to CIE Group employees in their business conduct.

The Code of Ethics applies to all the employees of the Group. Employees who are engaged in the purchasing of goods or services, the placement of contracts or the approval of payments to or by the Group must have particular regard to the terms of the Code.

Principles of the Code of Ethics

The guiding principles of the Code of Ethics can be summarised under four headings:

— Integrity
— Confidentiality
— Legality
— Disclosure of interest

Integrity

Each employee of the CIE Group is expected to observe the highest standards of honesty and integrity in all his/her business dealings.

To this end, as an employee, one must:

— refuse bribes, gifts or hospitality which may affect one's ability to make independent judgement, and report any such approaches in writing to one's superior
— avoid misrepresenting one's position or being ambiguously misleading
— reject any business practice which might reasonably be deemed to be improper
— not abuse one's position in the Company for personal gain

Confidentiality

Every employee in the CIE Group owes a duty of confidentiality to the Group. Employees are required to ensure that business information which they obtain by reason of their employment is not mis-used, whether by suppliers, their competitors or competitors of the CIE Group.

In order to protect such information, employees are required to:

— ensure that such information is properly safeguarded

— exercise due care in communicating such information
— avoid using such information for personal gain.

Employees are reminded that the Transport (Re-Organisation of Coras Iompair Eireann) Act, 1986, includes a specific duty not to disclose confidential information. Breach of this statutory duty is an offence.

Legality

In order to ensure compliance in one's business dealings with the laws of Ireland, employees are required to:

— fulfill all regulatory and supervisory obligations imposed on CIE
— co-operate with relevant regulatory and supervisory bodies
— avoid false, inaccurate or mis-leading entries in record
— ensure that taxation and welfare legislation is upheld
— ensure one's actions comply with relevant contractual obligations
— encourage effective and fair competition at all times
— comply with the Group purchasing and tendering procedures and with prescribed levels of authority for sanctioning any relevant expenditure
— avoid engaging in any illegal or criminal activities

Disclosure of Interest

All employees of the CIE Group are required to disclose in writing to the Head of Group Procurement, through their superiors, details of any conflict of interest which might affect their impartiality in carrying out their duties as soon as they become apparent, including:

— any interest, shareholding or possible conflict of interest an employee has with any firm or organisation from which the CIE Group purchases supplies, works or services, or through whom the CIE Group proposes to sell property or services

— any outside employment or business interests in conflict or potentially in conflict with CIE's business

— any interest of an employee's immediate family which could involve such a conflict of interest

Where a conflict of interest situation could arise for an employee, he/she must desist from dealing with the contract giving rise to that situation, and may not attempt in any way to influence the Company decision on the matter.

Guidelines regarding Gifts or Hospitality

It is customary for many suppliers to offer gifts, hospitality or entertainment to named employees with whom they have contact as a result of business dealings.

Gifts

Employees may accept gifts from suppliers to or contractors who have worked for the CIE Group , provided:

— the gift is unsolicited

— the gift is one of very small intrinsic value (eg diary, calendar, bottle of wine/spirits etc)

— the value of such gifts accepted in a year from any one source do not exceed •100

— the gift is disclosed to that employee's immediate superior

In all other cases, the gift should be returned to the sender, with a note advising that acceptance would be contrary to Group policy. Details of returned gifts must be notified at once to the recipient's superior

Sponsorship requested on behalf of a club or society within the CIE Group from suppliers or contractors to CIE must not exceed in any year Euro 500 total value of sponsorship from such supplier or contractor unless the approval in writing of the Group Chief Executive is obtained.

Hospitality

Modest hospitality (including sporting events and golf outings) may be accepted, provided:

- — the frequency and scale of hospitality is not more than CIE might be expected to give in return
- — the number of CIE staff availing of the hospitality is kept to a minimum
- — invitations do not include the provision of travel or overnight accommodation and availing of the hospitality does not identify the CIE Group in a public way with any particular supplier or contractor.

3

International Association of Hospitality Advisors (IAHA): Code of Conduct

> If anyone tell thee that he has searched for knowledge and not attained it, believe him not; if he tell thee that he has attained knowledge without searching for it, believe him not; but if he tell thee that he has searched for knowledge and attained it, thou mayest believe him.
>
> —*The Talmud*

Preamble

The International Association of Hospitality Advisors was founded in recognition of the public need for competent, unbiased advice, professional guidance and sound judgment on the many diversified problems encountered in the hospitality industry.

The Association believes that by clearly recognizing the consulting function as a profession, and by organising the collective knowledge and experience of those engaged in hospitality consulting, the quality of consulting services to the industry will be greatly enhanced. Members of the Association have demonstrated their integrity and are qualified by their experience, training and knowledge to develop and express sound judgement on issues in the hospitality industry.

This Code is designed to serve notice to the public that members will assume the obligation of self-discipline above and beyond the requirements of law and that members will maintain a high level of ethics and professional service. The

Association enforces the Code by receiving and investigating all complaints of violations and by taking disciplinary action, including censure, suspension, or revocation of membership against any member who is found to be guilty of code violation or who willfully supports the practice of code violation.

It is a desire for the respect and confidence of the hospitality industry and of society that should motivate the consultant, or member, to maintain the highest possible ethical conduct. The loss of that respect and confidence is the ultimate sanction.

In recognition of the public interest in their obligation to the profession, members of the Association must agree in writing to comply with the following articles of professional conduct.

I. Professional Attitude and Behaviour

A member of the International Association of Hospitality Advisors shall conduct all professional activities in a manner that reflects credit upon the member, the Association, and the hospitality industry.

1. Members will not take personal, financial or other advantage of inside material or information resulting from their professional relationship with clients unless proper, full disclosure has been made; nor will they provide the basis on which others might take such advantage.

2. Members will not advertise their services in misleading language or any other manner that could be detrimental to the respect and honor afforded the Association or its individual members.

3. Members will not solicit employees of clients for employment except with the consent of the client.

4. Members shall maintain and improve their professional competence by continually devoting the necessary time to reading appropriate professional literature, participating in

educational seminars and programmes in their field and pursuing other continuing professional education activities.

5. Members will endeavor to assist those who enter the hospitality industry consulting profession in acquiring a full understanding of the ethics, processes, responsibilities and competencies of the profession and by keeping them informed of significant advances in their areas of practice.

6. Members will support this Code by reporting code violations to the Association in accordance with the established procedures for handling the alleged violations of the Code of Professional Conduct of the International Association of Hospitality Advisors.

II. Relationships with Clients

A member of the International Association of Hospitality Advisors must not accept any assignment or engage in any practice involving a violation of the law, this Code or the member's specific ethical responsibilities. A member must immediately withdraw from any assignment if such a violation is identified.

A. General Responsibilities

1. Members shall, before accepting an engagement, confer with the client or prospective client in sufficient detail and gather sufficient facts to gain an understanding of the perceived issues, the objectives to be achieved, the scope of assistance needed and the possible benefits that may accrue to the client.

2. Members will hold as strictly confidential all information concerning the affairs of the client that is gathered during the course of a professional engagement except when the client has released such information.

3. Members will advise the client of any significant reservations they have regarding anticipated benefits of an engagement. They will not accept an engagement in which they cannot perceive a client benefit.

4. Members will not promise any benefit that is not within their control to deliver.

B. Independence, Objectivity, and Integrity

1. Members will assume an independent position with the client, making certain that advice to clients is based on impartial consideration of all pertinent facts and responsible opinions. Members will not knowingly present a misleading report.

2. A member must not accept any assignment involving a conflict of interest and must withdraw from an assignment when an unavoidable conflict of interest arises after the assignment has been accepted unless such conflict is fully disclosed in writing to all parties and all parties agree that the assignment may be accepted or continued.

3. A member must not knowingly accept any assignment in which the member is called upon solely to lend professional reputation or signature to misleading predetermined opinions or positions.

4. A member must not accept any assignment which precludes or limits the ability to develop factual and supportable opinions, findings or conclusions. If the client requests the scope of the assignment to be limited (to the extent that the consultant may not be able to consider all relevant factors), then these limitations must be communicated in writing and agreed upon by the client before accepting the assignment.

C. Arrangements with Clients

1. The valuation of services and the procedures by which fees are charged are matters of individual preference and are based upon agreement between the consultant and client. However, members will agree with the client in advance on the basis for charges, including the reimbursement of expenses.

2. A member is precluded from accepting a contingency fee in situations where the member is represented or reasonably expected to be independent for the purposes of completing the project, unless such engagement arrangements are disclosed in writing in all communications with third parties.

D. Due Professional Care/Competency Provision

1. A member may not accept any assignment which is beyond the scope of the member's competency, knowledge and expertise unless the member obtains the needed knowledge or expertise from other sources.

2. Members will ensure that others they assign to an engagement, including subcontractors, comply with the standards set out herein, are qualified to produce the engagement benefits and are adequately supervised.

3. Members will ensure that sufficient relevant information is obtained and evaluated in developing conclusions and recommendations.

4. Members will perform each engagement on an individualized basis and will develop recommendations designed specifically to address each client's issues. Such solutions should be realistic and practical, clearly understood by the client and capable of being implemented by the client.

5. Members will demonstrate a commitment to the quality of their advice, assistance and resulting services through sufficient planning, reviews and controls.

III. Professional Relationships

Members of the International Association of Hospitality Advisors recognize that from time to time they will be working with other professional hospitality consultants as well as those from other disciplines and that it is necessary to adhere to certain standards of conduct in order to maximize the benefits to clients as well as to maintain the professional relationships within the profession.

1. Members recognize their responsibility to the profession to share with their colleagues the general body of knowledge and nonproprietary approaches they use in serving clients.

2. Members referring another consultant to a client will not misrepresent the qualifications of the other consultant nor will they make any commitments for the other consultant. Members receiving a referral from another will ensure that no misrepresentations or commitments have been made.

3. When engaged by a client to review the work of another consultant who is a member of this Association, members will exercise objectivity and integrity in all technical and advisory conclusions communicated to a client.

IV. Procedures for Handling Alleged Violations of Code of Professional Conduct

The purposes of the procedures are to provide a mechanism for determining the merits of complaints against members in a fair hearing before an unbiased tribunal; to protect the rights, privacy, and professional reputations of members; and to protect the rights and interests of clients in dealing with members.

1. Any person, member or nonmember, may file a charge of misconduct against a member. Misconduct is deemed to be any violation of the Code of Professional Conduct. The charge may be formal or informal.

2. A formal charge is a written statement of the facts alleged, with substantiating evidence, copies of which the Chairman transmits to the Professional Conduct Committee and to the accused member, identifying the party who filed the complaint. After investigation, the committee decides whether to dismiss the charge or refer the matter with recommendations to the Board of Directors for hearing and decision.

3. Upon receipt of an informal complaint of misconduct on the part of a member, the Chairman initiates a confidential

inquiry to confirm its substance. If there is reasonable ground for the complaint, the chairman formulates a statement of charges, to which the accused member may file an explanation or rebuttal within 30 days. If the Chairman of the Professional Conduct Committee and the Association Chairman jointly determine that the charges are sufficiently serious, the whole Committee will review the matter and recommend one of the following courses: dismiss the complaint; instruct the Chairman to obtain additional information required to arrive at a decision; instruct the Chairman to send a letter to the offending member in the nature of a warning or immediate cease and desist order. If the same violation occurs after a cease and desist order has been communicated to a member, a formal charge will be entered against the offending member.

4. The Board of Directors serves as an unbiased judicial tribunal, hearing testimony provided by the Professional Conduct Committee and the accused member. A member of the Board of Directors may have a conflict to serve as an unbiased member on a judicial tribunal; in this case, a member appointed by the Board may fill the Board position. All individuals serving on a judicial tribunal must sign a nonconflict form. The Board's decision, by majority vote, may take the form of dismissal of the complaint without prejudice, a letter of censure from the President, suspension from the Association for a stated period, or expulsion of the member from the Association.

5. All matters relative to the filing and investigation of charges or complaints are regarded as confidential and are not in any way made public until the final step in these procedures has been completed. If a committee member breaches the confidentiality, he or she shall be disciplined.

6. When a member withdraws from membership or is removed from the Association, he or she will immediately:

a. Return the Certificate of Membership and Association pin to the Association office.

b. Cease to use the International Association of Hospitality Advisors designation in association with his or her name, reports, or any other communications.

c. No longer hold himself or herself out as a member of the International Association of Hospitality Advisors.

International Association of Hospitality Advisors By-Laws

Article 1: Name

The name of this organisation shall be the "International Association of Hospitality Advisors."

Article 2: Purpose

The Association is founded as an association of professional individuals dedicated to the advancement of the hospitality industry.

The mission of the Association is to advance the profession of consulting within the hospitality industry by enhancing the quality of services provided to clients, by influencing related industries and by providing a vehicle for recognition of its members. To this end, the Association:

1. Promotes high standards in the conduct of hospitality consulting as evidenced by the Association's Code of Professional Conduct;

2. Serves as a resource of special skills and expertise;

3. Serves as a support body for the profession; and

4. Anticipates and responds to present and future needs and uses within the hospitality industry.

Article 3: Membership

A. Classes of Membership

1. The Association shall be composed of individuals, not organisations.

2. Two classes of membership shall be established: Member and Honorary Member.

3. Admission to membership shall be through the Membership Committee and according to criteria and procedures established by the Membership Committee and approved by the Board from time to time.

4. Individuals who continue to meet the requirements for each class of membership and have been voted into membership shall have equal rights as set forth below by member class.

B. Members

1. Candidates for membership shall be individuals only, not organisations, corporations or groups.

2. An invitation for membership shall be by written form, which form shall include not less than a signed agreement to abide by the Code of Professional Conduct and such professional and character references and other professional and personal information as the Membership Committee shall from time to time require.

3. Each candidate shall be sponsored by an active Member acquainted with the work and reputation of the candidate.

4. Each sponsor shall submit in writing the specific reasons why he or she is recommending the individual as a candidate for membership.

5. Sponsors of a candidate shall be excluded from serving on the Membership Screening subcommittee for that candidate.

6. The Membership Committee, through its screening subcommittee, shall:

a. Check references and conduct a personal interview with the candidate.

b. Review two specific assignments undertaken in the past two years.

c. The Board directs the Membership Committee to submit all screened candidates to the Board for approval prior to submission of the candidacy to the membership for vote. Board approval shall require an 80 percent vote of the Board quorum.

7. Admission shall be by an 80 percent vote of a membership quorum.

8. Criteria for admission as a Member are:

a. Practicing hospitality consultant for three consecutive years immediately preceding invitation or two consecutive years if candidate has ten years of hospitality experience or experience in his or her respective profession;
b. Primary professional activity is as a practicing hospitality industry consultant;
c. Sale of a service as opposed to a product;
d. Service to a minimum of three clients within the past twelve months immediately preceding the invitation;
e. Being an employee, owner, officer, partner or principal of his or her company;
f. Demonstrated competence in the field as defined by the Board from time to time;
g. "Practicing hospitality consultant" means an individual who is fully professionally occupied in the provision of hospitality consulting services;
h. Qualification may be waived by the Board for candidates who are full-time faculty, holding full Professor standing, at an accredited four-year institution of higher learning, and who teach hospitality-related courses;
i. "Consulting services" means professional advisory services for which the individual is fully and

unconditionally compensated on an industry-competitive basis.

9. From time to time the Board may limit the number of candidates approved for membership on an annual basis.

10. The Board of Directors may, from time to time, limit membership of certain professional disciplines.

11. It is recommended that each candidate for membership attend a semiannual meeting prior to approval as a Member.

12. All Members shall have rights to participate in and vote at all regular and special meetings of the Association and shall be eligible for board or officer positions of the Association.

13. The Board of Directors shall adopt a policy for continuing education requirements for Members to maintain active membership within IAHA. Such policy shall be determined by the Board and may change from time to time.

C. Honorary Members

1. Honorary membership shall be by vote of three-quarters of the Members to extend an invitation to such persons that the Board of Directors has deemed to be in the best interest of the Association for such persons' contribution to the hospitality industry or the hospitality consulting profession.

2. Honorary membership election shall be for life, unless otherwise so determined by the Board.

3. The number of Honorary Members may vary at the discretion of the Board of Directors

D. Retention of Membership

An individual shall retain membership by the timely paying of dues, continuing as a practicing hospitality consultant, as defined in B.8.g. above, and by remaining in compliance with the criteria appropriate to the individual's class of membership as such criteria are from time to time established by the Board.

E. Termination of Membership

Voluntary termination shall be by resignation in writing to the Board. Involuntary termination shall be in writing to the Member for cause upon a three-fourths vote by the Board in accordance with the Code of Professional Conduct; except, however, in the event that involuntary termination is on the basis that the Member no longer meets the criteria for membership; then no finding of cause shall be required.

F. Reinstatement of Membership

1. A Member who has voluntarily terminated membership may reapply for membership and may be readmitted on a three-fourths vote of the Board, excluding other membership application processes.

2. A Member of any class whose membership has been involuntarily terminated for cause may reapply for membership of that class following two years and unanimous vote of the Board.

3. A Member whose membership has been terminated for failure to meet the criteria for membership may reapply for membership when again able to meet the criteria for membership.

Article 4. Dues

Annual membership dues shall be such amount as determined by the Board from time to time. There shall be no dues for Honorary Members.

Dues are payable annually on January 1 for the upcoming year; dues past due for more than sixty days shall constitute failure to meet the criteria for membership.

Candidates for membership shall pay a candidacy fee, to be established by the Board from time to time, to cover the cost of the invitation process.

Article 5: Officers

A. Positions

1. The officers shall include the Chairman, President, Executive Vice-President, Secretary, Treasurer, and such additional Vice-Presidents as the Board may from time to time create.

2. The Chairman, President, Executive Vice-President, Secretary, and Treasurer shall be members of the Board of Directors.

B. Election

1. The officers shall be nominated from the Members by the Nominating Committee and elected by a simple majority of the membership for a term of one year or until their successors are elected and installed; except, however, the term of the Treasurer shall be for two years and the President shall in effect have a term of two years in that he or she automatically becomes Chairman upon completion of the term as President.

2. A vacancy in an officership shall be filled by the simple majority vote of the Board of Directors for the unexpired term or until the successor is elected and installed.

3. The officers shall assume their duties at the close of the annual meeting of the membership at which they are elected.

C. Duties

1. Chairman

   a. The Chairman shall be the immediate past President.
   b. The Chairman shall preside at the meetings of the Board and at the annual meeting, shall be an ex-officio member of all committees and shall be Chairman of the Nominating Committee.

2. President

   a. The President shall be the Chief Executive Officer of

the Association, shall be ex-officio Member of all committees and shall perform and direct such other activities as the Board may from time to time approve.

b. The President may, upon Board approval, delegate the day-to-day tasks of the office to a paid Executive Director and/or professionally certified association management firm.

3. Executive Vice-President

The Executive Vice-President shall assist the President and assume the duties of the President in the absence of the President. The Executive Vice-President is an ex-officio Member of all committees and shall perform such other duties as the Board may from time to time direct.

4. Secretary

The Secretary shall be responsible for keeping, maintaining and disseminating all internal and external nonfinancial corporate communications of the Association as well as all non-financial minutes and records.

5. Treasurer

The Treasurer shall be custodian of the funds of the Association, shall be responsible for keeping and maintaining the books and records and disseminating all internal and external financial information of the Association, and shall share responsibility with the President for preparation and presentation of the annual budget of the Association at the annual meeting.

6. Removal of An Officer

An officer may be removed only for cause and that by:

a. A three-fourths vote of the Board of Directors; or

b. A two-thirds vote of the Members, whether assembled or by proxy.

Article 6. Board of Directors

A. Eligibility for Membership

Any Member in good standing shall be entitled to be elected a Member of the Board of Directors; except, however, no more than one Board Member shall be from the same firm or organisation.

B. Nomination

The Nominating Committee shall present a slate of at least one candidate for each vacancy to be filled on the Board of Directors, which slate shall be published in writing to the membership not less than ninety days prior to the annual meeting. In addition, nominations may be made from the floor at the annual meeting.

C. Election

The Board of Directors may be elected by the adoption of the slate presented by the Nominating Committee. In the case of floor nomination or multiple nominations for single openings by the Nominating Committee, then voting shall be by Board opening with secret ballot.

D. Term and Composition of Board

1. Terms on the Board shall be for three years, with division as evenly as the number of Members allows; except, however, the term of the Treasurer shall always be two years and the President shall effectively have a two-year term by automatically becoming Chairman following his or her term as President.

2. The Board of Directors shall be comprised of the officers and eight directors. There shall be two non-U.S. Members as constituents of the eight directors. If a non-U.S. Members is unable to attend a meeting, his or her proxy shall automatically be given to the Chairman first, and the President second.

E. Duties

The Board of Directors shall have full authority to direct the operation of the Association consistent with these By-Laws and the laws of the State of Florida. The Board may appoint, delegate and otherwise authorize others to act in its behalf and may compensate such others for so doing.

F. Vacancies

Vacancies among directors may be filled by majority vote of the remaining Members of the Board. Persons so elected shall serve the unexpired term or until the successor shall be elected and installed.

G. Removal of Directors

A director may be removed for cause only and for that by:

1. A three-fourths vote of the Board of Directors, or

2. A two-thirds vote of the Members, whether assembled or by proxy.

3. In the event that a director does not attend two regularly scheduled Board Meetings within that director's term, the Board shall vote as to whether that nonattending Member shall be removed for cause.

H. Meetings of the Board

1. Board meetings shall be at the annual meeting and at such other times as the business of the Association shall require.

2. Meetings may be by telephone.

3. Special meetings of the Board may be called by the Chairman.

I. Quorum

1. A majority of the Board shall constitute a quorum.

2. Each Member of the Board shall have one vote, and a simple majority of those present and voting at the meeting shall decide all questions, unless a higher-percentage vote is required for specific types of questions specified elsewhere in these By-Laws.

Article 7. Committees

A. Standing Committees

The standing Committees shall be Membership, Nominating, Professional Conduct, and Marketing.

B. Standing Committee Composition

1. With the exception of the Nominating Committee, the President shall appoint the Chairman of each standing committee. The Chairman of the Board shall be the Chairman of the Nominating Committee. The Chairman of a standing committee shall select the members of that committee with the approval of the Board.

2. No committee's composition shall include more than one person from any firm or organisation.

C. Special Committees

The Board or the Chairman may appoint special committees from time to time.

D. Committee Operation

Committees shall direct and manage their affairs according to these By-Laws and the rules and procedures established by the Board.

Article 8. Membership Meetings

A. Annual Meetings

The annual meeting shall be held at such time and place as the Board shall set at the immediately preceding annual meeting.

B. Special Meetings

1. Special meetings of the membership may be held at the call of the Board or the majority of the membership following thirty days written notice.

2. Any business of the Association may be conducted at a special meeting; provided, however, that such business is set out in writing in the notice of the meeting.

C. Other Meetings

The Association may hold such other additional meetings from time to time as the Board approves

D. Quorum

A simple majority of the membership shall constitute a quorum for any meeting of the membership.

E. Voting

Each Member shall have one vote, and a simple majority of those present and voting or returning a mail ballot shall decide all questions, except that it shall require a two-thirds vote of the Members to reverse a Board action, to amend the By-Laws, or to remove a director. Approval for membership shall require an 80 percent vote of a membership quorum.

F. Record of Meetings

1. Any called meeting of Members of the Association shall be recorded in minutes. Except in the case of a meeting other than the annual meeting held not more than thirty days prior to the request, such minutes shall be provided within fifteen (15) days of their request to any Member of the Association.

2. The Minutes of the annual meeting of the Association shall be circulated to the membership within sixty days of the close of the annual meeting.

Article 9. Fiscal Year

The fiscal year of the Association shall be a calendar year.

Article X. Indemnification

Any officer, director or Member acting by or on behalf of the Association in a Board-approved manner shall be defended and held harmless by the Association to the extent of its funds and any insurance, which insurance shall be obtained as soon as the Association is able, against any action or proceeding of any kind, provided only that the action taken by such officer, director or Member was taken in good faith.

Article XI. Dissolution

In the event of dissolution of the Association and after payment of all debts and other obligations, the assets of this Association shall be dedicated or transferred only in accordance with the purposes set out herein and the laws of the State of Florida.

The unanimous vote of the Board and three-quarters of the Members shall be required to dissolve the Association.

Article XII. Amendemnts and Rules of Order

A. Amendments

These By-Laws may be amended by two-thirds vote of the Members at a regular or special meeting or mail ballot, provided only that such proposed amendment and the reasons therefor shall have been submitted to the membership in writing not less than thirty days prior to the date of the vote.

B. Rules of Order

"Robert's Rules of Order Newly Revised' shall be the rules of parliamentary procedure governing the conduct of all meetings of the Association not otherwise provided for in these By-Laws.

4

Workplace: Problem of Ethics and Discrimination

> The best preacher is the heart; the best teacher is time; the best book is the world; the best friend is God.
>
> —*The Talmud*

I

HOSPITALITY INDUSTRY: SEXUAL HARASSMENT ISSUES

Sexual harassment is not easy to define. Individuals have different perceptions as to what constitutes sexual harassment and a definition is almost impossible to construct. (Federal Register, 1980). The following provides some insight into what constitutes sexual harassment.

The European Commission Code of Practice defines sexual harassment as:

> Unwanted conduct of a sexual nature, or other conduct based on sex affecting the dignity of women and men at work. This can include unwelcome physical, verbal or non-verbal conduct. *The Equal Employment Opportunity Commission* (EEOC) - a federal agency in charge of enforcing sexual harassment guidelines in the USA - provides a threefold guideline of sexual harassment, interpreted from Title VII of the Civil Rights Act of 1964.

— sexual advances;

— for sexual favours;
— verbal or physical conduct of a sexual nature where:
— submission to it is explicitly or implicitly a term or condition of an individual's employment;
— submission to or rejection of such conduct by an individual is used as the basis for employment decisions affecting such individual; or
— such conduct has the purpose or effect of unreasonably interfering with an individual's work performance or creating an intimidating, hostile or offensive working environment.

In the UK, the Criminal Justice and Public Order Act 1994 renders racial, sexual and other forms of harassment in the street, at home, and at work, a criminal offence punishable by imprisonment—up to six months—and/or a fine not exceeding £5,000. The Act creates a new offence of intentional harassment, and covers other forms of harassment on grounds such as sex, disability, age and sexual orientation. A person is guilty of an offence if he or she, with intent, causes another person harassment, alarm or distress by: using threatening, abusive or insulting words or behaviour, or disorderly behaviour; or displaying any writing, sign or other visible representation which is threatening, abusive or insulting. In addition to prosecuting the harasser under criminal law, a UK employee can also seek redress from an Industrial Tribunal, as sexual harassment can amount to unlawful sex discrimination against males or females under the Sex Discrimination Act 1975.

An Understanding of Harassment

Recent research by Head *et al.* (1995) examines the variable factors that may have a determining impact on the perception of sexual harassment—specifically, gender and management status of the perpetrator, and the education level of the evaluator. The research suggests that education level does have an impact on perception of harassment whereby the more educated the employees are, the less tolerant they become. The lower tolerance of educated women is also identified by Gutek (1993). Folgero and Fjeldstad (1995) discuss the concept of traditional work capacities of reproduction and production roles of women and men, and apply this as a partially causal effect of sexual harassment. The feminisation of particular jobs may lead to attitudes toward what is expected of service employees in terms of remarks that can be made or level of personal contact which is acceptable.

Another cause of differing perceptions is the hierarchical status of the perpetrator in relation to the victim. It has been suggested that the perceived seriousness of the behaviour increases with the power of the person making the advances. The Head *et al.* (1995) research purports that whether a behaviour is perceived to be sexually harassing or not, will be a function of both the organisational hierarchical position of the perpetrator, and the gender of both parties. Their results indicate that when comparing identical behaviours, the actions of male superiors are most construed to be sexually harassing, while female peers' actions are least construed to be sexually harassing.

Measuring the Problem of Sexual Harassment

The true extent of sexual harassment is often disguised by the conspiracy of silence which shrouds the issue, with the victim often leaving the company to escape the harassment without providing the organisation with the true reason for leaving. To provide a contemporary overview of sexual harassment in the Hospitality Industry the authors contacted 220 personnel directors.

A list was compiled utilising the *Hospitality Yearbook 1997* directory of companies. A self-completion questionnaire and letter explaining the research was mailed to personnel directors. The response rate was 32 companies (14.5 per cent) with almost one third having less than 100 employees, one third 100-500 employees and one third over 500 employees.

Determining which behaviours actually constitute sexual harassment is perhaps the most complex and controversial aspect of the issue. Within groups, even for women, there does not appear to be agreement as to what constitutes sexual harassment. According to a survey in 1990 (Davidson and Earnshaw, 1990) of British management's attitudes to sexual harassment in the workplace, only 64.8 percent of respondents regarded sexual harassment as a serious management issue.

The findings from our survey are slightly different as they show that while almost 1 in 5 treat sexual harassment as a minor issue the majority (75 per cent) of the hospitality industry respondents treat such a situation as of critical importance. It was reported that 90 per cent of the companies which responded provide staff training/induction courses relating to appropriate and inappropriate conduct in the workplace when dealing with customers. This training consists of written information (87 per cent), seminars (36 per cent), meetings (65 per cent), notice boards (45 per cent) and videotapes (23 per cent). Respondents were also asked their views as to the way in which their Company views sexual harassment of service staff by customers. Given the earlier importance reported for the seriousness of sexual harassment in the workplace it would not seem that companies are as positive about policies or the need to provide help for staff in dealing with problems. There is some ambiguity as to what constitutes sexual harassment issues.

The following provides evidence of what is considered serious. The seeming acceptability by a high number of companies of sexual teasing, jokes and remarks; or sexually suggestive looks and gestures, may mask a hostile work environment where perpetrators are seen as Don Juans rather than wrongdoers. The interpretational element of sexual harassment means that actions that seem harmless or amusing to managers may be viewed as offensive and harassing to hospitality service staff.

Sexual Harassment in Hospitality and Service Organisations

The inherent characteristics of service organisations create a prime breeding ground for sexual harassment. By its nature, the service production process is inextricably linked to the close involvement of the customer, and behavioural norms are often set around satisfying a customer's expectations; preferably exceeding those expectations. In addition to the intra-organisational strains resulting from the "normal" conflicts between different hierarchical levels and departments, the service organisation has to deal with three categories of workers: back-stage staff, front-line personnel, and participating customers. The constant interaction between these groups is therefore a constant source of stress and conflict. The service workplace is largely populated by women, especially at the lower levels. Service employees tend to be young and have little formal education. Their position in the workplace is often weak: young women are less confident when dealing with people in authority, and feel less important than any other group of employees in the work place (Aaron and Dry, 1992; Hamilton and Veglahn, 1992; Laudadio, 1988). Due to the lack of legitimate, coercive, reward, or expert power, the service worker may have to rely on referent power; that is, to be socially attractive and friendly with the customer. One author knows of a young girl who was told on starting as a waitress to "wear her skirt as short as she would feel it comfortable".

Research by Eller (1990) clearly indicates that more men and women experience sexual harassment in the hotel industry than do individuals in society-at-large. Woods and Kavanagh (1994) also found that hospitality managers perceive sexual harassment to be pervasive within the industry.

The hospitality industry may be particularly susceptible to incidents of sexual harassment due to the ambiguity of "hospitality service" , the unusual hours and conditions of work, the interaction of persons in the delivery of service, and the importance placed on appearance—which focuses attention on people as sexual beings. In many customer contact roles in the service sector, "sexiness" is a part of the role itself, the "job flirt" is encouraged as a part of the service style (Hall, 1993) and there may be a thin line between "selling the service" and "selling sexuality". We found from our hospitality survey of personnel directors that 80 per cent responded that the dress code was important with 39 per cent allowing very short skirts and 38 per cent not allowing trousers.

Interestingly on being asked if safe "flirting" with customers was part of the job for your service staff 7 per cent agreed it was and 39 per cent were neutral. Outlets such as TGI Fridays utilise training schemes which encourage flirtation as a means of increasing the amount spent and repeat business. This is not an easy situation to manage. MacKinnon (1979), for example, defines the role of the waitress as requiring "constant vigilance, skillful obsequiousness, and an ability to project the implication that there (are) ... sexual possibilities for the relationship while avoiding the explicit 'how about it' that would force a refusal into the open". While management may implicitly or explicitly encourage customer contact staff to use their personality (sexuality) to please the customer, the staff themselves may also actively exploit their assets for their own interests.

The following quotation (Cook, 1996) from a London waitress demonstrates some of the contradictions of the role: Everyone I know wears shorter skirts ... especially on Saturday nights - because you can guarantee better tips ... I suppose you are slightly willing to compromise and I'm not as feminist about it as I know I should be. But unfortunately men tip and women don't. An emphasis on the quality of customer service, which is normally regarded as a positive feature of an organisation, may leave staff feeling unsupported and vulnerable if they are expected to respond in a reasonable and friendly manner to customers who overstep the mark. Hochschild's (1983) classic study of cabin attendants showed the stress associated with having to keep smiling regardless of the way one is treated by customers. Sosteric (1996) reports a case study of staff in a night-club whose morale and quality of service went down when they were no longer allowed, in the name of improving customer service, to support each other and use aggression and rudeness to deal with obnoxious behaviour or sexual harassment from customers. Unlike office and manufacturing work places where an employee works virtually without interruption from outsiders, hotel employees usually have close social contact with co-workers, supervisors, customers and suppliers. Moreover, hotel employees work long, irregular hours and experience periods of intense activity balanced with slack periods. These long hours often involve night, evening and even holiday shifts. In an environment of heightened - almost forced - social interaction (particularly in smaller hotels with shared employee accommodation), a prime breeding ground exists for the existence of sexual harassment.

Maintaining a stable workforce has become a critical success factor in sustaining a competitive advantage. Service organisations - particularly the hotel industry - presently face intense staff turnover, high labour costs, and a diminishing supply of workers. Of our sample, 58 per cent reported fairly high turnover rates and 23 per cent high rates. 19 per cent of companies reported staff had resigned due to harassment by customers and 23 per cent could not say one way or another if this was a reason. Continually having to be polite and friendly towards offensive customers, and lack of power to control one's own working environment, can lead to a feeling of "burnoutness" and alienation. The ultimate result of such feelings may be that the employee leaves the organisation. Alternatively, and as damaging to the organisation, the employee may withdraw psychologically and go through the motions of "being nice to the customers" with smiles eliding into sneers (Filby, 1992).

Sexual harassment also presents economic, social and competitive issues for a company. A successful company requires the existence of good relations among its employees and the people with whom the company does business. Sexual harassment creates poor working relationships which can harm the company, the individuals directly involved, and indirectly, other employees within the company. Additional problems will exist within organisational relationships: companies which have "high rates of sexual harassment also have high rates of racial harassment, discrimination, and other forms of unfair treatment" (Sandroff, 1992). This finding indicates that companies which tolerate sexual harassment tend to have personnel problems in general.

The cost of sexual harassment to businesses is one that should not be overlooked. In 1988, *Working Women* magazine surveyed 160 of the "Fortune 500" manufacturing and service companies in the US, representing 3.3 million employees (Sandroff, 1992) and found an average company loss of $6.7 million a year in decreased productivity, increased absenteeism and higher employee turnover caused by sexual harassment. Despite these tangible financial or economic costs, the "real" or underlying costs to businesses and human suffering may be immeasurable.

One of the most disturbing consequences of sexual harassment is the human impact, with devastating short- and long-term physical and psychological consequences. We found that 10 per cent of our hospitality industry sample had been involved in legal proceedings following an incidence of sexual harassment by a customer or member of staff. Many victims suffer "...detrimental physical and psychosocial effects ranging from sickness, anger, anxiety, tiredness, fear, sleep problems, weight loss, relationship problems, depression and loss of confidence, to nervous breakdown" (Earnshaw and Davidson, 1994). Not surprisingly, the victim's relationship with others (particularly other men - if the harasser was a man) can also be adversely affected (Gutek, 1985) as can a victims' general attitude towards work in terms of lowered motivation, decreased job satisfaction, lowered confidence to do the job and lowered organisational commitment.

Two-thirds of sexual harassment complaints in America's largest corporations were made against immediate supervisors and upper management. This finding raises a very serious concern, because it is the responsibility of management to implement programmes designed to reduce the occurrence of sexual harassment. This point stresses the need for a company policy that allows a variety of channels through which harassment claims can be filed, allowing one's immediate supervisor or manager to be by-passed (Barton and Eichelberger, 1994). A formalised procedure for creating a policy, that will assist hospitality managers in preparing a response to the problem of sexual harassment., Victims are unlikely to report incidents unless they are sure that their complaints will be dealt with seriously and sympathetically.

Therefore, the most important aspect of a sexual harassment policy is the firm and continued commitment from senior management to encourage the creation of an open culture which has preventive measures. This requires clearly defined anti-sexual policies with well displayed information on ways of confidential reporting; to take all reports seriously and ensuring that immediate corrective action is taken against the perpetrator(s) of sexual harassment.

Such an approach opens up the organisation to a monitoring of the extent of any problems related to sexual harassment. In addition this will enhance equal opportunities and guard against future legal claims. It will also provide a clear message to all hospitality employees about the company's ethical position with regard to staff, management and its customers.

While the type of formal policy described above is undoubtedly beneficial, it should be recognised that a formal policy alone may not solve all problems. Sexuality is an inevitable part of organisational life and in many service roles staff are encouraged to use their sexuality to please customers and sell the product although most employers would not openly admit this. Of course staff are often encouraged to "flirt" and not to genuinely "come on" but it is hardly surprising if the distinction between the role and the reality can become blurred and staff can often be left to feel that it is their responsibility alone to keep control of the situation as the following quote from a waitress working at a novelty restaurant in London which attracts groups of drunken "City boys" illustrates: All the girls here are very broadminded. It goes with the turf. Inevitably you are going to be groped at some stage but it is up to you to control the situation. One comment is usually enough to stop them doing it (Cook, 1996). Rather than focusing merely on mechanisms for reporting and dealing with sexual harassment when it has happened, managers need to be aware of the way their strategies (the service styles they define, the type of clientele they attract) impact on their staff.

It is unrealistic and repressive to suggest that one should never use sex to sell, but, if one does, the organisation has a responsibility to ensure that staff are supported and protected against unacceptable behaviour from customers. The maximisation of profit remains a pivotal objective for service business activity and as such organisations need to deal proactively with the issue of sexual harassment.

This organisational view of treating sexual harassment as a matter of employee effectiveness places the locus on preventative management and protection of the most fundamental resource of the company - the personal resource. A service company requires a happy and well motivated workforce in order to be successful. By systematically removing the occurrence of sexual harassment, organisations can meet both the employee's need for protection, and the organisational need for productivity and effectiveness.

II

SEXUAL HARASSMENT POLICY & HOSPITALITY SECTOR

Two-thirds of sexual harassment complaints in America's largest corporations were made against immediate supervisors and upper management. This finding raises a very serious concern, because it is the responsibility of management to implement programmes designed to reduce the occurrence of sexual harassment. This point stresses the need for a company policy that allows a variety of channels through which harassment claims can be filed, allowing one's immediate supervisor or manager to be by-passed (Barton and Eichelberger, 1994). A formalised procedure for creating a policy, that will assist hospitality managers in preparing a response to the problem of sexual harassment., Victims are unlikely to report incidents unless they are sure that their complaints will be dealt with seriously and sympathetically.

Therefore, the most important aspect of a sexual harassment policy is the firm and continued commitment from senior management to encourage the creation of an open culture which has preventive measures. This requires clearly defined anti-sexual policies with well displayed information on ways of confidential reporting; to take all reports seriously and ensuring that immediate corrective action is taken against the perpetrator(s) of sexual harassment.

Such an approach opens up the organisation to a monitoring of the extent of any problems related to sexual harassment. In addition this will enhance equal opportunities and guard against future legal claims. It will also provide a clear message to all hospitality employees about the company's ethical position with regard to staff, management and its customers.

While the type of formal policy described above is undoubtedly beneficial, it should be recognised that a formal policy alone may not solve all problems. Sexuality is an inevitable part of organisational life and in many service roles staff are encouraged to use their sexuality to please customers and sell the product although most employers would not openly admit this.

Of course staff are often encouraged to "flirt" and not to genuinely "come on" but it is hardly surprising if the distinction between the role and the reality can become blurred and staff can often be left to feel that it is their responsibility alone to keep control of the situation as the following quote from a waitress working at a novelty restaurant in London which attracts groups of drunken "City boys" illustrates: All the girls here are very broadminded. It goes with the turf. Inevitably you are going to be groped at some stage but it is up to you to control the situation.

One comment is usually enough to stop them doing it (Cook, 1996). Rather than focusing merely on mechanisms for reporting and dealing with sexual harassment when it has happened, managers need to be aware of the way their strategies (the service styles they define, the type of clientele they attract) impact on their staff. It is unrealistic and repressive to suggest that one should never use sex to sell, but, if one does, the organisation has a responsibility to ensure that staff are supported and protected against unacceptable behaviour from customers.

The maximisation of profit remains a pivotal objective for service business activity and as such organisations need to deal proactively with the issue of sexual harassment. This organisational view of treating sexual harassment as a matter of employee effectiveness places the locus on preventative management and protection of the most fundamental resource of the company—the personal resource.

A service company requires a happy and well motivated workforce in order to be successful. By systematically removing the occurrence of sexual harassment, organisations can meet both the employee's need for protection, and the organisational need for productivity and effectiveness.

III

SEXUAL HARASSMENT IN HOSPITALITY AND SERVICE ORGANISATIONS

The inherent characteristics of service organisations create a prime breeding ground for sexual harassment. By its nature, the service production process is inextricably linked to the close involvement of the customer, and behavioural norms are often set around satisfying a customer's expectations; preferably exceeding those expectations. In addition to the intra-organisational strains resulting from the "normal" conflicts between different hierarchical levels and departments, the service organisation has to deal with three categories of workers: back-stage staff, front-line personnel, and participating customers. The constant interaction between these groups is therefore a constant source of stress and conflict.

The service workplace is largely populated by women, especially at the lower levels. Service employees tend to be young and have little formal education. Their position in the workplace is often weak: young women are less confident when dealing with people in authority, and feel less important than any other group of employees in the work place (Aaron and Dry, 1992; Hamilton and Veglahn, 1992; Laudadio, 1988). Due to the lack of legitimate, coercive, reward, or expert power, the service worker may have to rely on referent power; that is, to be socially attractive and friendly with the customer.

One author knows of a young girl who was told on starting as a waitress to "wear her skirt as short as she would feel it comfortable". Research by Eller (1990) clearly indicates that more men and women experience sexual harassment in the hotel industry than do individuals in society-at-large. Woods and Kavanagh (1994) also found that hospitality managers perceive sexual harassment to be pervasive within the industry.

The hospitality industry may be particularly susceptible to incidents of sexual harassment due to the ambiguity of "hospitality service" , the unusual hours and conditions of work, the interaction of persons in the delivery of service, and the importance placed on appearance—which focuses attention on people as sexual beings. In many customer contact roles in the service sector, "sexiness" is a part of the role itself, the "job flirt" is encouraged as a part of the service style (Hall, 1993) and there may be a thin line between "selling the service" and "selling sexuality". We found from our hospitality survey of personnel directors that 80 per cent responded that the dress code was important with 39 per cent allowing very short skirts and 38 per cent not allowing trousers.

Interestingly on being asked if safe "flirting" with customers was part of the job for your service staff 7 per cent agreed it was and 39 per cent were neutral. Outlets such as TGI Fridays utilise training schemes which encourage flirtation as a means of increasing the amount spent and repeat business. This is not an easy situation to manage. MacKinnon (1979), for example, defines the role of the waitress as requiring "constant vigilance, skillful obsequiousness, and an ability to project the implication that there (are) ... sexual possibilities for the relationship while avoiding the explicit 'how about it' that would force a refusal into the open". While management may implicitly or explicitly encourage customer contact staff to use their personality (sexuality) to please the customer, the staff themselves may also actively exploit their assets for their own interests.

The following quotation (Cook, 1996) from a London waitress demonstrates some of the contradictions of the role: Everyone I know wears shorter skirts ... especially on Saturday nights—because you can guarantee better tips ... I suppose you are slightly willing to compromise and I'm not as feminist about it as I know I should be. But unfortunately men tip and women don't. An emphasis on the quality of customer service, which is normally regarded as a positive feature of an organisation, may leave staff feeling unsupported and vulnerable if they are expected to respond in a reasonable and friendly manner to customers who overstep the mark. Hochschild's (1983) classic study of cabin attendants showed the stress associated with having to keep smiling regardless of the way one is treated by customers. Sosteric (1996) reports a case study of staff in a night-club whose morale and quality of service went down when they were no longer allowed, in the name of improving customer service, to support each other and use aggression and rudeness to deal with obnoxious behaviour or sexual harassment from customers. Unlike office and manufacturing work places where an employee works virtually without interruption from outsiders, hotel employees usually have close social contact with co-workers, supervisors, customers and suppliers.

Moreover, hotel employees work long, irregular hours and experience periods of intense activity balanced with slack periods. These long hours often involve night, evening and even holiday shifts. In an environment of heightened—almost forced—social interaction (particularly in smaller hotels with shared employee accommodation), a prime breeding ground exists for the existence of sexual harassment.

IV

FULL IMPACT OF SEXUAL HARASSMENT IN HOSPITALITY INDUSTRY

Maintaining a stable workforce has become a critical success factor in sustaining a competitive advantage. Service organisations—particularly the hotel industry—presently face intense staff turnover, high labour costs, and a diminishing supply of workers. Of our sample, 58 per cent reported fairly high turnover rates and 23 per cent high rates. 19 per cent of companies reported staff had resigned due to harassment by customers and 23 per cent could not say one way or another if this was a reason. Continually having to be polite and friendly towards offensive customers, and lack of power to control one's own working environment, can lead to a feeling of "burnoutness" and alienation. The ultimate result of such feelings may be that the employee leaves the organisation. Alternatively, and as damaging to the organisation, the employee may withdraw psychologically and go through the motions of "being nice to the customers" with smiles eliding into sneers (Filby, 1992).

Sexual harassment also presents economic, social and competitive issues for a company. A successful company requires the existence of good relations among its employees and the people with whom the company does business. Sexual harassment creates poor working relationships which can harm the company, the individuals directly involved, and indirectly, other employees within the company. Additional problems will exist within organisational relationships: companies which have "high rates of sexual harassment also have high rates of racial harassment, discrimination, and other forms of unfair treatment" (Sandroff, 1992). This finding indicates that companies which tolerate sexual harassment tend to have personnel problems in general.

The cost of sexual harassment to businesses is one that should not be overlooked. In 1988, *Working Women* magazine surveyed 160 of the "Fortune 500" manufacturing and service companies in the US, representing 3.3 million employees (Sandroff, 1992) and found an average company loss of $6.7 million a year in decreased productivity, increased absenteeism and higher employee turnover caused by sexual harassment. Despite these tangible financial or economic costs, the "real" or underlying costs to businesses and human suffering may be immeasurable.

One of the most disturbing consequences of sexual harassment is the human impact, with devastating short- and long-term physical and psychological consequences. We found that 10 per cent of our hospitality industry sample had been involved in legal proceedings following an incidence of sexual harassment by a customer or member of staff.

Many victims suffer "...detrimental physical and psychosocial effects ranging from sickness, anger, anxiety, tiredness, fear, sleep problems, weight loss, relationship problems, depression and loss of confidence, to nervous breakdown" (Earnshaw and Davidson, 1994). Not surprisingly, the victim's relationship with others (particularly other men—if the harasser was a man) can also be adversely affected (Gutek, 1985) as can a victims' general attitude towards work in terms of lowered motivation, decreased job satisfaction, lowered confidence to do the job and lowered organisational commitment.

5

Hotel Ethics Management

> It is rare that the public sentiment decides immorally or unwisely, and the individual who differs from it ought to distrust and examine well his own opinion.
>
> —*Thomas Jefferson*

Unfortunately, far too many resources about business ethics end up being designed primarily for philosophers, academics and social critics. As a result, leaders and managers struggle to really be able to make use of the resources at all. Also, far too many resources about business ethics contain sensationalistic stories about businesses "gone bad" or prolonged preaching to businesses to "do the right thing". These resources often explore simplistic ethical questions, such as "Should Jane steal from the company?" The real world of leaders and managers is often much more complex than that. This guide is a straightforward and highly practical tool designed to help leaders and managers implement comprehensive ethics management systems in their workplaces — systems to deal with the complex, ethical issues that can occur in the day-to-day realities of leading and managing an organisation.

For Web readers: This free guidebook is about 20 pages long. If you are reading the document on the www, please wait until the document is fully loaded before attempting to link to its sections listed below. The best approach to using this guidebook may be to print it out for ongoing reference. The Free Management Library provides additional information about ethics and a great range of other free information about management.

Disclaimer: The author, Carter McNamara, MBA, PhD, makes no warranty, express or implied, nor assumes any legal liability for accuracy, completeness, or usefulness of any information from this guide.

Another Tool to Effectively Infuse Ethical Principles: If you are planning to infuse strong, ethical principles throughout your company or want to change the culture of your company, then you might take the advice of Bob Kniffin, Vice President of External Affairs, at Johnson and Johnson (J&J) company. The way that J&J handled an ethical issue (the "Tylenol scare" crisis) in the 1980s is probably one of the most inspiring and enlightening examples of how to successfully deal with a major ethical issue in business. Kniffin was one of the key players in helping J&J to handle the crisis so effectively. Kniffin said that it was not the J&J Credo (a form of a code of ethics) that helped J&J to handle the crisis so well. Rather, it was the ongoing "challenge sessions" that the company regularly held in order for each person to clarify their own perspective and commitment to the J&J Credo. Authenticity Consulting's peer coaching groups are a powerful, yet straightforward, means to organise, facilitate and evaluate challenge sessions.

About this Free Guidebook

- *This free guidebook aims to fill a large void of practical, realistic ethics information for leaders and managers,* whether nonprofit or for-profit.
- *This guidebook takes about two hours to read.* It is concisely written and well organised as a step-by-step guidebook for handy reference.
- *This guidebook is free in order to make its contents highly accessible to organisations,* particularly those with limited resources. The free nature of this document does not in any way indicate that its content are of low value — high fees and impressive presentation do not necessarily imply high value.

— *The author hopes the on-line form of this document remains a dynamic community resource* that is continually modified and improved by feedback, particularly from leaders and managers—those people in the trenches who are charged with applying business ethics techniques in the workplace.

This document contains the following sections:

1. Document Fills a Void of Practical Business Ethics Information for Leaders and Managers

Current Literature is Focused on Needs of Philosophers, Academics and Social Critics —

Leaders and Managers Require More Practical Information About Managing Ethics

Managing ethics in the workplace holds tremendous benefit for leaders and managers, benefits both moral and practical. This is particularly true today when it is critical to understand and manage highly diverse values in the workplace.

However, the field of business ethics has traditionally been the domain of philosophers, academics and social critics. Consequently, much of today's literature about business ethics is not geared toward the practical needs of leaders and managers — the people primarily responsible for managing ethics in the workplace. The most frequent forms of business ethics literature today typically include: a) philosophical, which requires extensive orientation and analysis; b) anthologies, which require much time, review and integration; c) case studies, which require numerous cases, and much time and analyses to synthesize; and d) focus on social responsibility, which includes many examples of good and bad actions taken by companies. (This lack of practical information is not the fault of philosophers, academic or social critics. The problem is the outcome of insufficient involvement of leaders and managers in discussion and literature about business ethics. More leaders and managers must become involved. This guidebook aims to increase that involvement.)

What's Conspicuously Missing is the "How to" of Managing Ethics in the Workplace

But it isn't from lack of examples that managers aren't better at managing ethics in the workplace — they require more practical information about managing ethics. This problem was explained very well by Stark in his article, "What's the Matter with Business Ethics?" published in the *Harvard Business Review* (1993, May/June, pp. 38-48). Brenner (*Journal of Business Ethics,* V11, pp. 391:399) notes "while much has been written about individual components of ethics programmes, especially about codes of ethics, the literature is much more limited on ethics programmes." Wong and Beckman (*Journal of Business Ethics*, V11, pp. 173-178) note that "researchers are claiming that current literature is filled with strong arguments for more ethical corporate leadership and incorporation of ethics in business curriculum, but what is conspicuously missing is the "how to" in actually putting ethical goals and theories into practical action."

Myths Abound About Business Ethics, e.g., "Ethics is Simply to Do What's Right"

Lack of involvement from leaders and managers in the field of business ethics (again, this is the fault of no one or of everyone) has spawned a great deal of confusion and misunderstanding among leaders and managers about business ethics. McDonald and Zepp, in their article "What Should Be Done? A Practical Approach to Business Ethics" (*Management Decision*, 28, 1, 1990, pp. 9-13), note that when someone brings up the topic of business ethics "... it tends to bring up cynicism, righteousness, paranoia, and laughter." Many leaders and managers believe business ethics is religion because it seems to contain a great deal of preaching. Or, they believe it to be superfluous because it seems to merely assert the obvious: "do good!"

Business Ethics Literature is Often Far Too Simplistic — So Many Leaders and Managers Think Business Ethics is Irrelevant

Stark notes that "often ethicists advance a kind of moral absolutism that avoids many of the difficult and most interesting questions." Case studies to explore ethical dilemmas are often far too simplistic, presented as if every real-life situation has a right and wrong e.g., "should I lie, cheat or steal?" Consequently, many managers believe business ethics is irrelevant because too much business ethics training avoids the real-to-life complexities in leading organisations. (This document contains samples of real-to-life, complex ethical dilemmas, in a subsection, "Examples of Real-to-Life Complex Ethical Dilemmas" in the upcoming section "Ethics Tools: Resolving Ethical Dilemmas.") Bob Dunn, President and CEO of San Francisco-based Business for Social Responsibility, explains, "Ethical decisions aren't as easy as they used to be. Now, they're the difference between right — and right." Preston Townley, in his speech "Business Ethics: Commitment to Tough Decisions" (*Vital Speeches*, January 1992, pp. 208-211), states that "... it ought to be fairly easy to choose between right and wrong by relying on principles, but business activity often demands that we select from alternatives that are neither wholly right or wholly wrong."

2. *What is Business Ethics?*

Let's Start With "What is ethics?" Simply put, ethics involves learning what is right or wrong, and then doing the right thing — but "the right thing" is not nearly as straightforward as conveyed in a great deal of business ethics literature. Most ethical dilemmas in the workplace are not simply a matter of "Should Bob steal from Jack?" or "Should Jack lie to his boss?"

(Many ethicists assert there's always a right thing to do based on moral principle, and others believe the right thing to do depends on the situation — ultimately it's up to the individual.) Many philosophers consider ethics to be the "science of conduct." Twin Cities consultants Doug Wallace and John Pekel (of the Twin Cities-based Fulcrum Group; 651-714-9033; e-mail at jonpekel@atti.com) explain that ethics includes the fundamental ground rules by which we live our lives. Philosophers have been discussing ethics for at least 2500 years, since the time of Socrates and Plato. Many ethicists consider emerging ethical beliefs to be "state of the art" legal matters, i.e., what becomes an ethical guideline today is often translated to a law, regulation or rule tomorrow. Values which guide how we ought to behave are considered moral values, e.g., values such as respect, honesty, fairness, responsibility, etc. Statements around how these values are applied are sometimes called moral or ethical principles.

So What is "Business Ethics"? The concept has come to mean various things to various people, but generally it's coming to know what it right or wrong in the workplace and doing what's right — this is in regard to effects of products/ services and in relationships with stakeholders. Wallace and Pekel explain that attention to business ethics is critical during times of fundamental change — times much like those faced now by businesses, both nonprofit or for-profit. In times of fundamental change, values that were previously taken for granted are now strongly questioned. Many of these values are no longer followed. Consequently, there is no clear moral compass to guide leaders through complex dilemmas about what is right or wrong. Attention to ethics in the workplace sensitizes leaders and staff to how they should act. Perhaps most important, attention to ethics in the workplaces helps ensure that when leaders and managers are struggling in times of crises and confusion, they retain a strong moral compass. However, attention to business ethics provides numerous other benefits, as well (these benefits are listed later in this document).

Note that many people react that business ethics, with its continuing attention to "doing the right thing," only asserts the obvious ("be good," "don't lie," etc.), and so these people don't take business ethics seriously. For many of us, these principles of the obvious can go right out the door during times of stress. Consequently, business ethics can be strong preventative medicine. Anyway, there are many other benefits of managing ethics in the workplace. These benefits are explained later in this document.

Two Broad Areas of Business Ethics

1. *Managerial mischief.* Madsen and Shafritz, in their book "Essentials of Business Ethics" (Penguin Books, 1990) further explain that "managerial mischief" includes "illegal, unethical, or questionable practices of individual managers or organisations, as well as the causes of such behaviours and remedies to eradicate them." There has been a great deal written about managerial mischief, leading many to believe that business ethics is merely a matter of preaching the basics of what is right and wrong. More often, though, business ethics is a matter of dealing with dilemmas that have no clear indication of what is right or wrong.

2. *Moral mazes.* The other broad area of business ethics is "moral mazes of management" and includes the numerous ethical problems that managers must deal with on a daily basis, such as potential conflicts of interest, wrongful use of resources, mismanagement of contracts and agreements, etc.

Business ethics is now a management discipline. Business ethics has come to be considered a management discipline, especially since the birth of the social responsibility movement in the 1960s. In that decade, social awareness movements raised expectations of businesses to use their massive financial and social influence to address social problems such as poverty, crime, environmental protection, equal rights, public health and improving education. An increasing number of people asserted that because businesses were making a profit from using our country's resources, these businesses owed it to our country to work to improve society. Many researchers, business schools and managers have recognized this broader constituency, and in their planning and operations have replaced the word "stockholder" with "stakeholder," meaning to include employees, customers, suppliers and the wider community.

The emergence of business ethics is similar to other management disciplines. For example, organisations realised that they needed to manage a more positive image to the public and so the recent discipline of public relations was born. Organisations realised they needed to better manage their human resources and so the recent discipline of human resources was born. As commerce became more complicated and dynamic, organisations realised they needed more guidance to ensure their dealings supported the common good and did not harm others — and so business ethics was born.

Note that 90% of business schools now provide some form of training in business ethics. Today, ethics in the workplace can be managed through use of codes of ethics, codes of conduct, roles of ethicists and ethics committees, policies and procedures, procedures to resolve ethical dilemmas, ethics training, etc.

3. 10 Myths About Business Ethics

Business ethics in the workplace is about prioritizing moral values for the workplace and ensuring behaviours are aligned with those values — it's values management. Yet, myths abound about business ethics. Some of these myths arise from general confusion about the notion of ethics. Other myths arise from narrow or simplistic views of ethical dilemmas.

1. *Myth: Business ethics is more a matter of religion than management.* Diane Kirrane, in "Managing Values: A Systematic Approach to Business Ethics," (*Training and Development Journal*, November 1990), asserts that "altering people's values or souls isn't the aim of an organisational ethics programme — managing values and conflict among them is ..."

2. *Myth: Our employees are ethical so we don't need attention to business ethics.* Most of the ethical dilemmas faced by managers in the workplace are highly complex. Wallace explains that one knows when they have a significant ethical conflict when there is presence of a) significant value conflicts among differing interests, b) real alternatives that are equality justifiable, and c) significant consequences on "stakeholders" in the situation. Kirrane mentions that when the topic of business ethics comes up, people are quick to speak of the Golden Rule, honesty and courtesy. But when presented with complex ethical dilemmas, most people realise there's a wide "gray area" when trying to apply ethical principles.

3. *Myth: Business ethics is a discipline best led by philosophers, academics and theologians.* Lack of involvement of leaders and managers in business ethics literature and discussions has led many to believe that business ethics is a fad or movement, having little to do with the day-to-day realities of running an organisation. They believe business ethics is primarily a complex philosophical debate or a religion. However, business ethics is a management discipline with a programmatic approach that includes several practical tools. Ethics management programmes have practical applications in other areas of management areas, as well. (These applications are listed later on in this document.)

4. *Myth: Business ethics is superfluous — it only asserts the obvious: "do good!"* Many people react that codes of ethics, or lists of ethical values to which the organisation aspires, are rather superfluous because they represent values to which everyone should naturally aspire. However, the value of a codes of ethics to an organisation is its priority and focus regarding certain ethical values in that workplace. For example, it's obvious that all people should be honest. However, if an organisation is struggling around continuing occasions of deceit in the workplace, a priority on honesty is very timely — and honesty should be listed in that organisation's code of ethics. Note that a code of ethics is an

organic instrument that changes with the needs of society and the organisation.

5. *Myth: Business ethics is a matter of the good guys preaching to the bad guys.* Some writers do seem to claim a moral high ground while lamenting the poor condition of business and its leaders. However, those people well versed in managing organisations realise that good people can take bad actions, particularly when stressed or confused. (Stress or confusion are not excuses for unethical actions — they are reasons.) Managing ethics in the workplace includes all of us working together to help each other remain ethical and to work through confusing and stressful ethical dilemmas.

6. *Myth: Business ethics in the new policeperson on the block.* Many believe business ethics is a recent phenomenon because of increased attention to the topic in popular and management literature. However, business ethics was written about even 2,000 years ago — at least since Cicero wrote about the topic in his *On Duties.* Business ethics has gotten more attention recently because of the social responsibility movement that started in the 1960s.

7. *Myth: Ethics can't be managed.* Actually, ethics is always "managed" — but, too often, indirectly. For example, the behaviour of the organisation's founder or current leader is a strong moral influence, or directive if you will, on behaviour or employees in the workplace. Strategic priorities (profit maximization, expanding marketshare, cutting costs, etc.) can be very strong influences on morality. Laws, regulations and rules directly influence behaviours to be more ethical, usually in a manner that improves the general good and/or minimizes harm to the community. Some are still skeptical about business ethics, believing you can't manage values in an organisation. Donaldson and Davis (*Management Decision,* V28, N6) note that management, after all, is a value system. Skeptics might consider the tremendous influence of several "codes of ethics," such as the "10 Commandments" in Christian religions or the U.S. Constitution. Codes can be very powerful in smaller "organisations" as well.

8. *Myth: Business ethics and social responsibility are the same thing.* The social responsibility movement is one aspect of the overall discipline of business ethics. Madsen and Shafritz refine the definition of business ethics to be: 1) an application of ethics to the corporate community, 2) a way to determine responsibility in business dealings, 3) the identification of important business and social issues, and 4) a critique of business. Items 3 and 4 are often matters of social responsibility. (There has been a great deal of public discussion and writing about items 3 and 4. However, there needs to be more written about items 1 and 2, about how business ethics can be managed.) Writings about social responsibility often do not address practical matters of managing ethics in the workplace, e.g., developing codes, updating polices and procedures, approaches to resolving ethical dilemmas, etc.

9. *Myth: Our organisation is not in trouble with the law, so we're ethical.* One can often be unethical, yet operate within the limits of the law, e.g., withhold information from superiors, fudge on budgets, constantly complain about others, etc. However, breaking the law often starts with unethical behaviour that has gone unnoticed. The "boil the frog" phenomena is a useful parable here: If you put a frog in hot water, it immediately jumps out. If you put a frog in cool water and slowly heat up the water, you can eventually boil the frog. The frog doesn't seem to notice the adverse change in its environment.

10. *Myth: Managing ethics in the workplace has little practical relevance.* Managing ethics in the workplace involves identifying and prioritizing values to guide behaviours in the organisation, and establishing associated policies and procedures to ensure those behaviours are conducted. One might call this "values management." Values management is also highly important in other management practices, e.g., managing diversity, Total Quality Management and strategic planning.

4.10 Benefits of Managing Ethics in the Workplace

Many people are used to reading or hearing of the moral benefits of attention to business ethics. However, there are other types of benefits, as well. The following list describes various types of benefits from managing ethics in the workplace.

1. *Attention to business ethics has substantially improved society.* A matter of decades ago, children in our country worked 16-hour days. Workers' limbs were torn off and disabled workers were condemned to poverty and often to starvation. Trusts controlled some markets to the extent that prices were fixed and small businesses choked out. Price fixing crippled normal market forces. Employees were terminated based on personalities. Influence was applied through intimidation and harassment. Then society reacted and demanded that businesses place high value on fairness and equal rights. Anti-trust laws were instituted. Government agencies were established. Unions were organised. Laws and regulations were established.

2. *Ethics programmes help maintain a moral course in turbulent times.* As noted earlier in this document, Wallace and Pekel explain that attention to business ethics is critical during times of fundamental change — times much like those faced now by businesses, both nonprofit or for-profit. During times of change, there is often no clear moral compass to guide leaders through complex conflicts about what is right or wrong. Continuing attention to ethics in the workplace sensitizes leaders and staff to how they want to act — consistently.

3. *Ethics programmes cultivate strong teamwork and productivity.* Ethics programmes align employee behaviours with those top priority ethical values preferred by leaders of the organisation. Usually, an organisation finds surprising disparity between its preferred values and the values actually reflected by behaviours in the workplace. Ongoing attention and dialogue regarding values in the workplace builds

openness, integrity and community — critical ingredients of strong teams in the workplace. Employees feel strong alignment between their values and those of the organisation. They react with strong motivation and performance.

4. *Ethics programmes support employee growth and meaning.* Attention to ethics in the workplace helps employees face reality, both good and bad — in the organisation and themselves. Employees feel full confidence they can admit and deal with whatever comes their way. Bennett, in his article "Unethical Behaviour, Stress Appear Linked" (*Wall Street Journal*, April 11, 1991, p. B1), explained that a consulting company tested a range of executives and managers. Their most striking finding: the more emotionally healthy executives, as measured on a battery of tests, the more likely they were to score high on ethics tests.

5. *Ethics programmes are an insurance policy — they help ensure that policies are legal.* There is an increasing number of lawsuits in regard to personnel matters and to effects of an organisation's services or products on stakeholders. As mentioned earlier in this document, ethical principles are often state-of-the-art legal matters. These principles are often applied to current, major ethical issues to become legislation. Attention to ethics ensures highly ethical policies and procedures in the workplace. It's far better to incur the cost of mechanisms to ensure ethical practices now than to incur costs of litigation later. A major intent of well-designed personnel policies is to ensure ethical treatment of employees, e.g., in matters of hiring, evaluating, disciplining, firing, etc. Drake and Drake (California Management Review, V16, pp. 107-123) note that "an employer can be subject to suit for breach of contract for failure to comply with any promise it made, so the gap between stated corporate culture and actual practice has significant legal, as well as ethical implications."

6. *Ethics programmes help avoid criminal acts "of omission" and can lower fines.* Ethics programmes tend to detect ethical

issues and violations early on so they can be reported or addressed. In some cases, when an organisation is aware of an actual or potential violation and does not report it to the appropriate authorities, this can be considered a criminal act, e.g., in business dealings with certain government agencies, such as the Defense Department. The recent Federal Sentencing Guidelines specify major penalties for various types of major ethics violations. However, the guidelines potentially lowers fines if an organisation has clearly made an effort to operate ethically.

7. *Ethics programmes help manage values associated with quality management, strategic planning and diversity management — this benefit needs far more attention.* Ethics programmes identify preferred values and ensuring organisational behaviours are aligned with those values. This effort includes recording the values, developing policies and procedures to align behaviours with preferred values, and then training all personnel about the policies and procedures. This overall effort is very useful for several other programmes in the workplace that require behaviours to be aligned with values, including quality management, strategic planning and diversity management. Total Quality Management includes high priority on certain operating values, e.g., trust among stakeholders, performance, reliability, measurement, and feedback. Eastman and Polaroid use ethics tools in their quality programmes to ensure integrity in their relationships with stakeholders. Ethics management techniques are highly useful for managing strategic values, e.g., expand marketshare, reduce costs, etc. McDonnell Douglas integrates their ethics programmes into their strategic planning process. Ethics management programmes are also useful in managing diversity. Diversity is much more than the color of people's skin — it's acknowledging different values and perspectives. Diversity programmes require recognizing and applying diverse values and perspectives — these activities are the basis of a sound ethics management programme.

8. *Ethics programmes promote a strong public image.* Attention to ethics is also strong public relations — admittedly, managing ethics should not be done primarily for reasons of public relations. But, frankly, the fact that an organisation regularly gives attention to its ethics can portray a strong positive to the public. People see those organisations as valuing people more than profit, as striving to operate with the utmost of integrity and honor. Aligning behaviour with values is critical to effective marketing and public relations programmes. Consider how Johnson and Johnson handled the Tylenol crisis versus how Exxon handled the oil spill in Alaska. Bob Dunn, President and CEO of San Francisco-based Business for Social Responsibility, puts it best: "Ethical values, consistently applied, are the cornerstones in building a commercially successful and socially responsible business."

9. *Overall benefits of ethics programmes:* Donaldson and Davis, in "Business Ethics? Yes, But What Can it Do for the Bottom Line?" (Management Decision, V28, N6, 1990) explain that managing ethical values in the workplace legitimizes managerial actions, strengthens the coherence and balance of the organisation's culture, improves trust in relationships between individuals and groups, supports greater consistency in standards and qualities of products, and cultivates greater sensitivity to the impact of the enterprise's values and messages.

10. *Last - and most — formal attention to ethics in the workplace is the right thing to do.*

5. One Description of a Highly Ethical Organisation

Mark Pastin, in *The Hard Problems of Management: Gaining the Ethics Edge* (Jossey-Bass, 1986), provides the following four principles for highly ethical organisations:

1. They are at ease interacting with diverse internal and external stakeholder groups. The groundrules of these firms make the good of these stakeholder groups part of the organisations' own good.

2. They are obsessed with fairness. Their groundrules emphasize that the other persons' interests count as much as their own.
3. Responsibility is individual rather than collective, with individuals assuming personal responsibility for actions of the organisation. These organisations' groundrules mandate that individuals are responsible to themselves.
4. They see their activities in terms of purpose. This purpose is a way of operating that members of the organisation highly value. And purpose ties the organisation to its environment.

Doug Wallace asserts the following characteristics of a high integrity organisation:

1. There exists a clear vision and picture of integrity throughout the organisation.
2. The vision is owned and embodied by top management, over time.
3. The reward system is aligned with the vision of integrity.
4. Policies and practices of the organisation are aligned with the vision; no mixed messages.
5. It is understood that every significant management decision has ethical value dimensions.
6. Everyone is expected to work through conflicting-stakeholder value perspectives.

6. Ethics Management Programmes: An Overview

About Ethics Management Programmes

Organisations can manage ethics in their workplaces by establishing an ethics management programme. Brian Schrag, Executive Secretary of the Association for Practical and Professional Ethics, clarifies. "Typically, ethics programmes convey corporate values, often using codes and policies to guide decisions and behaviour, and can include extensive training and evaluating, depending on the organisation. They provide guidance in ethical dilemmas." Rarely are two programmes alike.

"All organisations have ethics programmes, but most do not know that they do," wrote business ethics professor Stephen Brenner in the *Journal of Business Ethics* (1992, V11, pp. 391-399). "A corporate ethics programme is made up of values, policies and activities which impact the propriety of organisation behaviours."

Bob Dunn, President and CEO of San Francisco-based Business for Social Responsibility, adds: "Balancing competing values and reconciling them is a basic purpose of an ethics management programme. Business people need more practical tools and information to understand their values and how to manage them."

Benefits of Managing Ethics as a Programme

There are numerous benefits in formally managing ethics as a programme, rather than as a one-shot effort when it appears to be needed. Ethics programmes:

- Establish organisational roles to manage ethics
- Schedule ongoing assessment of ethics requirements
- Establish required operating values and behaviours
- Align organisational behaviours with operating values
- Develop awareness and sensitivity to ethical issues
- Integrate ethical guidelines to decision making
- Structure mechanisms to resolving ethical dilemmas
- Facilitate ongoing evaluation and updates to the programme
- Help convince employees that attention to ethics

is not just a knee-jerk reaction done to get out of trouble or improve public image

7. Guidelines for Managing Ethics in the Workplace

The following guidelines ensure the ethics management programme is operated in a meaningful fashion:

1. *Recognize that managing ethics is a process.* Ethics is a matter of values and associated behaviours. Values are discerned through the process of ongoing reflection. Therefore, ethics programmes may seem more process-oriented than most management practices. Managers tend to be skeptical of process-oriented activities, and instead prefer processes focused on deliverables with measurements. However, experienced managers realise that the deliverables of standard management practices (planning, organising, motivating, controlling) are only tangible representations of very process-oriented practices. For example, the process of strategic planning is much more important than the plan produced by the process. The same is true for ethics management. Ethics programmes do produce deliverables, e.g., codes, policies and procedures, budget items, meeting minutes, authorization forms, newsletters, etc. However, the most important aspect from an ethics management programme is the process of reflection and dialogue that produces these deliverables.
2. *The bottom line of an ethics programme is accomplishing preferred behaviours in the workplace.* As with any management practice, the most important outcome is behaviours preferred by the organisation. The best of ethical values and intentions are relatively meaningless unless they generate fair and just behaviours in the

workplace. That's why practices that generate lists of ethical values, or codes of ethics, must also generate policies, procedures and training that translate those values to appropriate behaviours.

3. *The best way to handle ethical dilemmas is to avoid their occurrence in the first place.* That's why practices such as developing codes of ethics and codes of conduct are so important. Their development sensitizes employees to ethical considerations and minimize the chances of unethical behaviour occurring in the first place.
4. *Make ethics decisions in groups, and make decisions public, as appropriate.* This usually produces better quality decisions by including diverse interests and perspectives, and increases the credibility of the decision process and outcome by reducing suspicion of unfair bias.
5. *Integrate ethics management with other management practices.* When developing the values statement during strategic planning, include ethical values preferred in the workplace. When developing personnel policies, reflect on what ethical values you'd like to be most prominent in the organisation's culture and then design policies to produce these behaviours.
6. *Use cross-functional teams when developing and implementing the ethics management programme.* It's vital that the organisation's employees feel a sense of participation and ownership in the programme if they are to adhere to its ethical values. Therefore, include employees in developing and operating the programme.
7. *Value forgiveness.* This may sound rather religious or preachy to some, but it's probably the most important component of any management practice.

An ethics management programme may at first actually increase the number of ethical issues to be dealt with because people are more sensitive to their occurrence. Consequently, there may be more occasions to address people's unethical behaviour. The most important ingredient for remaining ethical is trying to be ethical. Therefore, help people recognize and address their mistakes and then support them to continue to try operate ethically.

8. *Note that trying to operate ethically and making a few mistakes is better than not trying at all.* Some organisations have become widely known as operating in a highly ethical manner, e.g., Ben and Jerrys, Johnson and Johnson, Aveda, Hewlett Packard, etc. Unfortunately, it seems that when an organisation achieves this strong public image, it's placed on a pedestal by some business ethics writers. All organisations are comprised of people and people are not perfect. However, when a mistake is made by any of these organisations, the organisation has a long way to fall. In our increasingly critical society, these organisations are accused of being hypocritical and they are soon pilloried by social critics. Consequently, some leaders may fear sticking their necks out publicly to announce an ethics management programme. This is extremely unfortunate. It's the *trying* that counts and brings peace of mind — not achieving an heroic status in society.

8. Key Roles and Responsibilities in Ethics Management

Depending on the size of the organisation, certain roles may prove useful in managing ethics in the workplace. These can be full-time roles or part-time functions assumed by someone already in the organisation. Small organisations certainly will not have the resources to implement each the following roles using different people in the organisation.

However, the following functions points out responsibilities that should be included somewhere in the organisation.

1. *The organisation's chief executive must fully support the programme.* If the chief executive isn't fully behind the programme, employees will certainly notice — and this apparent hypocrisy may cause such cynicism that the organisation may be worse off than having no formal ethics programme at all. Therefore, the chief executive should announce the programme, and champion its development and implementation. Most important, the chief executive should consistently aspire to lead in an ethical manner. If a mistake is made, admit it.
2. *Consider establishing an ethics committee at the board level.* The committee would be charged to oversee development and operation of the ethics management programme.
3. *Consider establishing an ethics management committee.* It would be charged with implementing and administrating an ethics management programme, including administrating and training about policies and procedures, and resolving ethical dilemmas. The committee should be comprised of senior officers.
4. *Consider assigning / developing an ethics officer.* This role is becoming more common, particularly in larger and more progressive organisations. The ethics officer is usually trained about matters of ethics in the workplace, particularly about resolving ethical dilemmas.
5. *Consider establishing an ombudsperson.* The ombudsperson is responsible to help coordinate development of the policies and procedures to institutionalize moral values in the workplace. This position usually is directly responsible for

resolving ethical dilemmas by interpreting policies and procedures.

6. *Note that one person must ultimately be responsible for managing the ethics management programme.*

9. Ethics Tools: Codes of Ethics

About Codes of Ethics

According to Wallace, "A credo generally describes the highest values to which the company aspires to operate. It contains the `thou shalt's. A code of ethics specifies the ethical rules of operation. It's the `thou shalt not's." In the latter 1980s, The Conference Board, a leading business membership organisation, found that 76% of corporations surveyed had codes of ethics.

Some business ethicists disagree that codes have any value. Usually they explain that too much focus is put on the codes themselves, and that codes themselves are not influential in managing ethics in the workplace. Many ethicists note that it's the *developing* and *continuing dialogue* around the code's values that is most important.

Occasionally, employees react to codes with suspicion, believing the values are "motherhood and apple pie" and codes are for window dressing. But, when managing a complex issue, especially in a crisis, having a code is critical. More important, it's having *developed* a code. In the mid-70s, Johnson and Johnson updated their credo in a series of challenge meetings. Bob Kniffin, Vice President of External Affairs, explains, "We pored over each phrase and word. We asked ourselves, `Do we still believe this?' Our meetings resulted in some fine tuning, but basically we didn't change the values. The meetings infused the values in the minds of all of us managers." Many believe this process guided them in their well-known decision to pull Tylenol bottles off the shelves and repackage them at a $100 million expense. Kniffin offers some sound, practical advice. "In a crisis, there's no time for moral conclusions. Get those done beforehand. But also realise there's no substitute for sound crisis management. For example, have a list of people with fundamental knowledge, such as who transports your products where and when."

Developing Codes of Ethics

Note that if your organisation is quite large, e.g., includes several large programmes or departments, you may want to develop an overall corporate code of ethics and then a separate code to guide each of your programmes or departments.

Also note that codes should not be developed out of the Human Resource or Legal departments alone, as is too often done. Codes are insufficient if intended only to ensure that policies are legal. All staff must see the ethics programme being driven by top management.

Note that codes of ethics and codes of conduct may be the same in some organisations, depending on the organisation's culture and operations and on the ultimate level of specificity in the code(s).

Optional: Also see in the Free Management Library at http://www.managementhelp.org:

1. Organisational Culture - review to get a basic understanding of "personalities" of organisations
2. Strategic Planning - specific to developing a Values Statement
3. Valuing Diversity - to consider that there are other values and perspectives

Consider the following guidelines when developing codes of ethics:

1. *Review any values need to adhere to relevant laws and regulations;* this ensures your organisation is not (or is not near) breaking any of them. (If you are breaking any of them, you may be far better off to report this violation than to try hide the

problem. Often, a reported violation generates more leniency than outside detection of an unreported violation, particularly per the new Federal Sentencing Guidelines.) Increase priority on values that will help your organisation operate to avoid breaking these laws and to follow necessary regulations.

2. *Review which values produce the top three or four traits of a highly ethical and successful product or service in your area,* e.g., for accountants: objectivity, confidentiality, accuracy, etc. Identify which values produce behaviours that exhibit these traits.
3. *Identify values needed to address current issues in your workplace.* Appoint one or two key people to interview key staff to collect descriptions of major issues in the workplace. Collect descriptions of behaviours that produce the issues. Consider which of these issues is ethical in nature, e.g.., issues in regard to respect, fairness and honesty. Identify the behaviours needed to resolve these issues. Identify which values would generate those preferred behaviours. There may be values included here that some people would not deem as moral or ethical values, e.g., team-building and promptness, but for managers, these practical values may add more relevance and utility to a code of ethics.
4. *Identify any values needed, based on findings during strategic planning.* Review information from your SWOT analysis (identifying the organisation's strengths, weaknesses, opportunities and threats). What behaviours are needed to build on strengths, shore up weaknesses, take advantage of opportunities and guard against threats?
5. *Consider any top ethical values that might be prized by stakeholders.* For example, consider

expectations of employees, clients/customers, suppliers, funders, members of the local community, etc.

6. *Collect from the above steps, the top five to ten ethical values which are high priorities in your organisation (see item #7 below for examples).*
7. *Examples of ethical values might include* (the following list is the "Six Pillars of Character" developed by The Josephson Institute of Ethics, 310-306-1868):
   a) *Trustworthiness:* honesty, integrity, promise-keeping, loyalty
   b) *Respect:* autonomy, privacy, dignity, courtesy, tolerance, acceptance
   c) *Responsibility:* accountability, pursuit of excellence
   d) *Caring:* compassion, consideration, giving, sharing, kindness, loving
   e) *Justice and fairness:* procedural fairness, impartiality, consistency, equity, equality, due process
   f) *Civic virtue and citizenship:* law abiding, community service, protection of environment
8. *Compose your code of ethics; attempt to associate with each value, two example behaviours which reflect each value.* Critics of codes of ethics assert that they seem vacuous because many only list ethical values and don't clarify these values by associating examples of behaviours.
9. *Include wording that indicates all employees are expected to conform to the values stated in the code of ethics.* Add wording that indicates where employees can go if they have any questions.

10. *Obtain review from key members of the organisation.* Get input from as many members as possible.
11. *Announce and distribute the new code of ethics (unless you are waiting to announce it along with any new codes of conduct and associated policies and procedures).* Ensure each employee has a copy and post codes throughout the facility.
12. *Update the code at least once a year.* As stated several times in this document, the most important aspect of codes is developing them, not the code itself. Continued dialogue and reflection around ethical values produces ethical sensitivity and consensus. Therefore, revisit your codes at least once a year — preferably two or three times a year.
13. *(Note that you cannot include values and preferred behaviours for every possible ethical dilemma that might arise.* Your goal is to focus on the top ethical values needed in your organisation and to avoid potential ethical dilemmas that seem mostly likely to occur.)
14. *Examples of a code of ethics:* This example code was developed by MAP for Nonprofits (http://www.managementhelp.org/ethics/teamvalu.htm) in St. Paul. The code is geared specifically to guiding relations among staff.

Note that you may be better off to generate your own code of ethics from scratch rather than reviewing examples from other organisations. All ethical values are attractive to include in a code; however, you are most interested in those that provoke behaviours needed in your organisation at this time. You may want to include quite different ethical values next year.

10. Ethics Tools: Codes of Conduct

About Codes of Conduct

"Codes of conduct specify actions in the workplace and codes of ethics are general guides to decisions about those actions," explains Craig Nordlund, Associate General Counsel and Secretary at Hewlett Packard. He suggests that codes of conduct contain examples of appropriate behaviour to be meaningful.

The Conference Board found that codes of conduct are increasingly sophisticated and focused at lower levels in companies. Departments frequently have their own codes. Be careful, though. An organisation could be sued for breach of contract if its practices are not in accord with its policies. That's why legal departments should review codes of conduct and other ethics policies. Also, that's why it's critical for organisations to review their policies at least once a year to ensure they are in accordance with laws and regulations.

Optional: also see in the Free Management Library at http://www.managementhelp.org:

1. Employee Law - review major issues and topics to discern what behaviours to avoid in the workplace
2. Policies (Personnel) - review more specifics about what behaviours to avoid

Developing a Code of Conduct

Note that if your organisation is quite large, e.g., includes several large programmes or departments, you may want to develop an overall corporate code of conduct, and then a separate code to guide each of your programmes or departments. Consider the following guidelines when developing codes of conduct:

1. *Identify key behaviours needed to adhere to the ethical values proclaimed in your code of ethics,* including ethical values derived from review of

key laws and regulations, ethical behaviours needed in your product or service area, behaviours to address current issues in your workplace, and behaviours needed to reach strategic goals.

2. *Include wording that indicates all employees are expected to conform to the behaviours specified in the code of conduct.* Add wording that indicates where employees can go if they have any questions.
3. *Obtain review from key members of the organisation.* Be sure your legal department reviews the drafted code of conduct.
4. *Announce and distribute the new code of conduct* (unless you are waiting to announce it along with any associated policies and procedures). Ensure each employee has a copy and post codes in each employee's bay or office.
5. *(Note that you cannot include preferred behaviours for every possible ethical dilemma that might arise.)*
6. *Examples of topics typically addressed by codes of conduct include*: preferred style of dress, avoiding illegal drugs, following instructions of superiors, being reliable and prompt, maintaining confidentiality, not accepting personal gifts from stakeholders as a result of company role, avoiding racial or sexual discrimination, avoiding conflict of interest, complying with laws and regulations, not using organisation's property for personal use, not discriminating against race or age or sexual orientation, and reporting illegal or questionable activity. *Go beyond these traditional legalistic expectations in your codes — adhere to what's ethically sensitive in your organisation, as well.* (Note that, as with codes of ethics, you may be better off to generate your own code of conduct

from scratch rather than reviewing examples from other organisations.)

11. Ethics Tools: Policies and Procedures

Optional: also see in the Free Management Library at http://www.managementhelp.org:

Policies (Personnel) - review to understand how to develop and apply personnel policies:

1. *Update policies and procedures to produce behaviours preferred from the code of conduct,* including, e.g., personnel, job descriptions, performance appraisal forms, management-by-objectives expectations, standard forms, checklists, budget report formats, and other relevant control instruments to ensure conformance to the code of conduct. In doing so, try to avoid creating ethical dilemmas such as conflicts-of-interest or infringing on employee's individual rights.
2. *There are numerous examples of how organisations manage values through use of policies and procedures.* For example, we're most familiar with the value of social responsibility. To produce behaviour aligned with this value, organisations often institute policies such as recycling waste, donating to local charities, or paying employees to participate in community events. In another example, a high value on responsiveness to customers might be implemented by instituting policies to return phone calls or to repair defective equipment within a certain period of time. Consider the role of job descriptions and performance appraisals. For example, an advanced technology business will highly value technical knowledge, creativity and systems thinking. They use job

descriptions and performance appraisals to encourage behaviours aligned with these values, such as rewarding advanced degrees, patents, and analysis and design skills.

3. *Include policies and procedures to address ethical dilemmas.* See the next section, "Ethics Tools: Resolving Ethical Dilemmas," to select a method which is most appropriate to your organisation's culture and operations.
4. *Include policies and procedures to ensure training of employees about the ethics management programme.* See a following section, "Ethics Tools: Training."
5. *Include policies and procedures to reward ethical behaviour and impose consequences for unethical behaviour.*
6. *Include a grievance policy for employees to use to resolve disagreements with supervisors and staff.*
7. *Consider establishing an ethics "hotline."* This function might best be provided by an outside consultant, e.g., lawyer, clergyperson, etc. Or, provide an anonymous "tip" box in which personnel can report suspected unethical activities, and do so safely on an anonymous basis.
8. *Once a year, review all personnel policies and procedures.* If yours is a small organisation, consider including all staff during this review. Take a full day for all staff to review policies and procedures, and suggest changes.
9. *For guidance in establishing personnel policies, see the Guide to Personnel Management and Policies* (http://www.managementhelp.org/mgmnt/prsnlmnt.htm).

12. Ethics Tools: Resolving Ethical Dilemmas (with Real-to-Life Examples)

Definition of an Ethical Dilemma. Perhaps too often, business ethics is portrayed as a matter of resolving conflicts in which one option appears to be the clear choice. For example, case studies are often presented in which an employee is faced with whether or not to lie, steal, cheat, abuse another, break terms of a contract, etc. However, ethical dilemmas faced by managers are often more real-to-life and highly complex with no clear guidelines, whether in law or often in religion.

As noted earlier in this document, Doug Wallace, Twin Cities-based consultant, explains that one knows when they have a significant ethical conflict when there is presence of a) significant value conflicts among differing interests, b) real alternatives that are equality justifiable, and c) significant consequences on "stakeholders" in the situation.

An ethical dilemma exists when one is faced with having to make a choice among these alternatives.

Real-to-Life Examples of Complex Ethical Dilemmas

— "A customer (or client) asked for a product (or service) from us today. After telling him our price, he said he couldn't afford it. I know he could get it cheaper from a competitor. Should I tell him about the competitor — or let him go without getting what he needs? What should I do?"

— "Our company prides itself on its merit-based pay system. One of my employees has done a tremendous job all year, so he deserves strong recognition. However, he's already paid at the top of the salary range for his job grade and our company has too many people in the grade above him, so we can't promote him. What should I do?"

— "Our company prides itself on hiring minorities.

One Asian candidate fully fits the job requirements for our open position. However, we're concerned that our customers won't understand his limited command of the English language. What should I do?"

— "My top software designer suddenly refused to use our e-mail system. He explained to me that, as a Christian, he could not use a product built by a company that provided benefits to the partners of homosexual employees. He'd basically cut himself off from our team, creating a major obstacle to our product development. What should I do?"

— "My boss told me that one of my employees is among several others to be laid off soon, and that I'm not to tell my employee yet or he might tell the whole organisation which would soon be in an uproar. Meanwhile, I heard from my employee that he plans to buy braces for his daughter and a new carpet for his house. What should I do?"

— "My computer operator told me he'd noticed several personal letters printed from a computer that I was responsible to manage. While we had no specific policies then against personal use of company facilities, I was concerned. I approached the letter writer to discuss the situation. She told me she'd written the letters on her own time to practice using our word processor. What should I do?"

— "A fellow employee told me that he plans to quit the company in two months and start a new job which has been guaranteed to him. Meanwhile, my boss told me that he wasn't going to give me a new opportunity in our company because he was going to give it to my fellow employee now. What should I do?"

Optional: also see in the Free Management Library at http://www.managementhelp.org:

1. Feedback
2. Listening
3. Questioning
4. Conflict (interpersonal)
5. Negotiating
6. Valuing Diversity

3 Methods to Resolve Ethical Dilemmas

Organisations should develop and document a procedure for dealing with ethical dilemmas as they arise. Ideally, ethical dilemmas should be resolved by a group within the organisation, e.g., an ethics committee comprised of top leaders/managers and/or members of the board. Consider having staff members on the committee, as well. The following three methods can be used to address ethical dilemmas. Methods include an ethical checklist, a ten-step method and a list of key questions. (Note that The Golden Rule is probably the most common method to resolve ethical dilemmas. The rule exists in various forms in many of the world religions.)

Method One - Ethical Checklist

Twin Cities-based consultants, Doug Wallace and Jon Pekel, suggest the following ethical checklist to address ethical dilemmas. If necessary, revise your decision and action plan based on results of the this test.

13. Ethics Tools: Training

The ethics programme is essentially useless unless all staff members are trained about what it is, how it works and their roles in it. The nature of the system may invite suspicion if not handled openly and honestly. In addition, no matter how fair and up-to-date is a set of policies, the legal system will often interpret employee behaviour (rather than written policies) as de facto policy. Therefore, all staff must be aware of and act in full accordance with policies and procedures (this is true, whether policies and procedures are for ethics programmes or personnel management). This full accordance requires training about policies and procedures.

Training Basics for Supervisors and Learners

1. Orient new employees to the organisation's ethics programme during new-employee orientation.
2. Review the ethics management programme in management training experiences.
3. Involving staff in review of codes is strong ethics training.
4. Involving staff in review of policies (ethics and personnel policies) is strong ethics training.
5. One of the strongest forms of ethics training is practice in resolving complex ethical dilemmas. Have staff use any of the three ethical-dilemma-resolution methods in this guidebook and apply them to any of the real-to-life ethical dilemmas also listed in this guidebook.
6. Include ethical performance as a dimension in performance appraisals.
7. The best ethics trainer: Bill Goodman, Chief Human Resource Officer at Aveda, describes, "We start our training even in our job ads," then adds, "but the best trainer is the behaviour of our leaders."
8. zGive all staff a copy of this free "Complete Guide to Ethics Management."

6

Case Studies on Application of Ethics

> There is no difference between knowledge and temperance; for he who knows what is good and embraces it, who knows what is bad and avoids it, is learned and temperate. But they who know very well what ought to be done, and yet do quite otherwise, are ignorant and stupid.
>
> —*Socrates*

I

RESORT HOTEL ASSOCIATION—CODE OF ETHICS: A CASE STUDY

RHA is member driven and managed. As intermediaries between our member resorts and the companies that provide insurance coverage, we recognize that we must be bound by high standards of ethical conduct. Accordingly, it is our responsibility to RHA members:

- To ensure that insurance coverage will be provided by financially stable organisations.
- To ensure that coverages will be specifically designed to meet the needs of resort hotels.
- To provide adequate limits of coverage.
- To ensure that members' insurance claims are resolved in an equitable, timely and effective manner.

— To provide effective loss-control and risk-management services.
— To strive to make the association a superior insurance risk in the commercial marketplace.
— To adhere to the highest professional standards of conduct.
— To present to our members, accurately and honestly, all facts essential to their buying decisions.
— To maintain strict confidentiality of member information.
— To exemplify the best professional standards of this industry.

II

US MODEL OF RULES AND REGULATIONS GOVERNING THE EXHIBITS

Eligibility for Exhibiting

The following qualifications are required of all exhibitors at the 2006 ASHP Summer Meeting to be held at the Walt Disney World Swan and Dolphin Hotel:

1. Products or services displayed must further the educational purpose of the Summer Meeting and Exhibit Programme to provide an atmosphere conducive to exchanging information and views about pharmacy practice and health care in a professional manner.

2. Products or services must be related to the practice of pharmacy in health systems or other related facilities.

No Sales Policy

Because of the educational nature of the exhibit programme, socliciation of business, all order taking, selling activity, conferences in the interest of business and similar activity on the exhibit floor is expressly prohibited and will be strictly and actively inforced.

Assignment of Space

Booth space will be allocated in the sole and exclusive discretion of the ASHP with due regard to grouping of exhibitors and date which Contract for Exhibit Space was recieved. The ASHP reserves the right, in the best interest of the Exhibits, to relocate booth space other than selected by the exhibitor. The decision of the ASHP, with respect to allocation of booth space, will be final and binding upon all exhibitors.

Space

The exhibit booth arrangement is shown by the floorplan in this prospectus. Dimensions and locations of each are resonably accurate, but only warrented to be approximate. Floorplan revisions will take place periodically.

Contract for Exhibit Services

The Contract for Exhibit Space must be properly filled out and accompanied by a deposit in the amount of at least fifty percent (50%) of the rental for booth space or spaces requested. The deposit is non-refundable. If the Contract is accepted by the ASHP, it shall become binding upon both the ASHP and the exhibitor with respect to space assigned and the use, and all other matters included in the Contract and the Exhibit Rules and Regulations. ASHP will assign and confirm booth space to the exhibitor and credit the deposit paid against the monies due when the Contract is accepted. This rule applies also to on-site contracts for exhibit space.

The balance of the booth rental must be paid on or before March 27, 2006 at which time all payments are non-refundable. Should an exhibitor fail to comply with this rule, the ASHP has full authority to cancel any or all booth space assigned to the exhibitor. In such case the deposit provided for above shall be retained by ASHP as liquidated damages in consideration of ASHP holding the exhibit space for exhibitor. Exhibitors will not be permitted to install exhibit or furnish booth until full payment of the booth rental fee has been paid. Payments to ASHP are not deductible as charitable contributions for federal income tax purposes. However, they may be deductible under other provisions of the Internal Revenue Code.

Activity Within the Exhibit

Any activity within the Exhibits, including without limitation, distribution (for free or otherwise) of any literature, product or any other item must conform to the educational and professional nature and character of the Meeting. ASHP reserves the right to prohibit and require immediate cessation of any activity or distribution which, in ASHP's sole discretion, is determined not to conform to the educational nature of the Exhibits. ASHP will provide advance approval of activities and items upon request of an Exhibitor. The Society's decision to prohibit and require cessation of any activity will be in the sole and exclusive discretion of ASHP and be final.

Contests, lotteries, raffles, or games of chance are strictly prohibited. The rights, and benefits hereunder are personal to Exhibitor and may not be assigned without the express written consent of ASHP. All exhibits must conform strictly to the Rules and Regulations. The ASHP reserves the right to restrict any exhibit which might be considered undesirable. This restriction includes, but is not limited to, articles, conduct, dress of models, printed matter or anything objectionable to the Exhibit or Exhibit Programme as a whole.

Exhibit Badges

Employees designated by the exhibitor will be issued exhibit badges that will authorize such employees to enter the exhibit area during hours when it is open for exhibitors but not the public. Each exhibiting organisation will be given four (4) complimentary exhibit badges per 10' x 10' booth. These complimentary badges will permit access to the exhibit hall and include CE credit. Additional exhibit badges may be obtained for a fee of $75.00 each per badge issued above the (4) complimentary badges; no CE will be included for these additional badges. Exhibit personnel who want to register and recieve CE, but exceed the complimentary badge allotment, will be required to pay the appicable meeting registration rates. ASHP members will pay the member rate, nonmemebers will pay the nonmember rate, and all early and on-site registrations rates will apply. All exhibitor badge requests must be submitted online. Refer to the website for instructions and hours.

If you make changes to your exhibit personnel on-site, the new representative should be prepared to pay a fee of $75.00 per badge. This does not pertain to changes made in advance of the meeting. The deadline for personnel changes is June 16, 2006.

Termination of Meeting and Exhibit

Should the premises in which the ASHP Summer Meeting is to be held become, in the sole judgment of the ASHP, unfit for occupancy, or should the Meeting and Exhibit be materially interfered with by reason of a strike, picketing, boycott, embargo, injunction, war, riot, emergency declared by a government agency, or any other act beyond the control of the ASHP, the Contract for Exhibit Space may be terminated. The ASHP will not incur any liability for damages sustained by exhibitor as a result of such termination. In the event of such termination, the exhibitor expressly waives such liability and releases the ASHP from all claims for damages and agrees that the ASHP shall have no obligations except to refund to the exhibitors a pro-rated share of the aggregate amount received by the ASHP (as rental for exhibit space for said Exhibit), after deducting all costs and expenses in connection with such Exhibit, including a reasonable reserve for claims, such deductions being hereby specifically agreed to by the exhibitor.

Exhibitor Withdrawal

Withdrawal by any exhibitor will not be accepted unless

written notice of such withdrawal has been received no later than March 27, 2006, by the ASHP. All deposits are non-refundable. Any exhibitor who withdraws after said time allowed for withdrawal shall pay to ASHP, as liquidated damages, a sum of money equal to one hundred percent (100%) of the full price of said exhibitor's booth space. ASHP shall retain the full price of exhibitor's booth space as liquidated damages for any exhibitor who withdraws after March 28, 2006.

Arrangements of Exhibits

Standard booth backgrounds and side rails, decorated with fantasy draperies, and uniform two-line signs are provided without charge, if ordered by early May. Booth backgrounds are eight feet and divider rails are 33 inches in height. In the area four feet forward from the rear background of each booth, display material may be placed up to a height not exceeding eight feet from the building floor. In any portion of the booth beyond four feet from the rear background of the booth, all parts of the exhibit shall be placed not to exceed the height of the rail, which is 33 inches from the building floor. These restrictions apply to both standard and peninsula booth layouts. The height restriction for island booths is 16 ft. All exposed parts of a display must be finished. Exhibits not conforming to these specifications, or are otherwise found objectionable in the opinion of the ASHP, will be prohibited. ASHP reserves the right, in the best interest of the exhibit, to relocate selected space in areas other than that selected by exhibitor.

Installation, Staffing, and Dismantling of Exhibits

The Walt Disney World Swan and Dolphin Hotel has been reserved for exhibit installation during the following hours:

Friday, June 23	8:00 AM - 5:00 PM
Saturday, June 24	8:00 AM-5:00 PM
Sunday, June 25	8:00 AM - 5:00 PM

Exhibitors are encouraged to finalize minor booth preparations, display samples, etc., on Monday, June 26, after 8:00 AM. All exhibits must be operational by 10:30 AM, June 26. After this hour, no installation work will be permitted without special permission of the ASHP.

If erection of any exhibit has not started by 12:00 PM, Sunday, June 25, the ASHP shall order the exhibit to be erected and the exhibitor will be responsible for payment of expenses incurred.

Dismantling or packing of exhibits cannot begin earlier than 1:00 PM, June 28. All displays must be ready for removal from the exhibit hall no later than Midnight, June 29. Exhibitors will be charged Five Hundred ($500.00) Dollars per day or any part thereof after 5:00 PM, June 30 that the exhibit remains on the leased premises.

ASHP and the Walt Disney World Swan and Dolphin Hotel each reserve the right to disassemble exhibits and charge the exhibitor the above fee plus damages in event these exhibits are not dismantled in a timely manner causing exhibitor to remain on the premises beyond authorized times. ASHP and the Walt Disney World Swan and Dolphin Hotel each assume no obligation to undertake disassembly and assume no liability for any action in connection with this activity.

Contract Labor

Exhibitors may use contractors other than the Official Exhibit Contractor to set up, erect and dismantle exhibits if at least thirty (30) days prior to the first official move-in day, Exhibitor provides to ASHP and the Walt Disney World Swan and Dolphin Hotel a written statement of authorization for each such contractor in which the Exhibitor: gives the name and address of each contractor, and lists the name of the supervisor to be in attendance; assumes all responsibility for acts of its contractors and holds harmless ASHP and the Walt Disney World Swan and Dolphin Hotel for any loss or damage, including reasonable attorneys fees, arising from any act or omission of its contractors and further holds harmless ASHP and the Walt Disney World Swan and Dolphin Hotel from any injury to property of the contractors and the contractors' employees, subcontractors' agents and servants; guarantees compliance with any and all laws, ordinances or regulations, all union and convention center requirements; and guarantees all work will be coordinated through and subject to the direction of the Official Exhibit Contractor to assure orderly work-flow. Further, exhibitors must have onsite and provide to the Official Exhibit Contractor: certificate(s) of insurance for their contractor(s), naming the Walt Disney World Swan and Dolphin Hotel and ASHP as an additional insured, this insurance shall afford immediate defense and indemnification, and the limit of the coverage must be no less than $1,000,000 combined single-limit bodily injury and broad-form property damage, including broad-form contractual liability. Contractors must strictly comply with the foregoing or they will not be permitted on the premises.

Exhibit Hours

Monday, June 26	11:00 AM - 2:00 PM
Tuesday, June 27	11:00 AM - 2:00 PM
Wednesday, June 28	11:00 AM - 1:00 PM

Staffing of Exhibits

Exhibit booths must be staffed during all exhibit hours by qualified employees of the exhibiting company who must be able to explain or demonstrate the products or services on display. Exhibitor assumes all responsibility for its exhibit personnel, employees, contractors, servants, agents, and for all persons admitted to the exhibit area using its Exhibitor's badge. All exhibitors are responsible for informing their own personnel and authorized representatives of these rules and regulations.

Music

Exhibitors shall not play or perform any music at any time without written approval from the Exhibits Manager. Notwithstanding the foregoing, Exhibitor represents and warrants that no musical work protected by copyright will be staged, produced, or otherwise performed, via either "live" or mechanical" means, by or on behalf of the Exhibitor at the Summer Meeting unless the Exhibitor has previously obtained written permission from the copyright owner, or the copyright owner's designee, (e.g., ASCAP, BMI, or SESAC) for such use. Exhibitor further represents and warrants that it shall be fully responsible for the performance of all obligations under any agreement permitting the use of such music, including but not limited to all obligations to report data and to pay royalty fees. Exhibitor agrees to indemnify, save and hold harmless ASHP and its directors, officers, agents, employees, and each of them, from and against any and all claims, costs and expenses (including legal fees and expenses) demands, actions and liabilities of every kind and character whatsoever with respect to any breach of the foregoing representations and warranties.

An exhibitor's service kit and/or CD-ROM providing information about ordering drayage, electrical services, furniture rental, labor, lead retrieval devices, etc., with a complete list of charges, will be mailed to exhibitors in April. Kits are mailed to the person listed on the exhibit contract. Kit and CD-ROM information will be available online.

Care of Exhibit Space and Premises

The exhibitor, at his own expense, shall install carpet in his exhibit space, shall take good care of his exhibit space, not deface or mar said premises and will keep and maintain the aforesaid premises in good order at all times. Decorations may not be taped, nailed, tacked, or otherwise fastened to the ceilings, painted surfaces, columns, fabrics or walls. Exhibitors may not distribute adhesive backed decals/stickers inside the Walt Disney World Swan and Dolphin Hotel or on the premises. Electrical or other mechanical apparatus must be muffled so noise does not interfere with other exhibitors.

Exhibitors will not mar, deface or otherwise damage any area or equipment of the Walt Disney World Swan and Dolphin Hotel.

Safety

No combustible decoration, such as crepe paper, tissue paper, cardboard, or corrugated paper shall be used at any time. All packing containers, excelsior and wrapping paper should all be removed from the floor and must not be stored under tables or behind displays. All muslin, velvet, silken or any other cloth decorations must stand a flameproof test as prescribed by the fire ordinance of the City of Orlando and Orange County. Volatile, explosive or other flammable matter, or any substances prohibited by the law or insurance carriers, are not permitted on premises.

All electrical equipment must meet applicable National Electrical Codes requirements of the Walt Siney World Swan and Dolphin Hotel. Electrical fixtures and fittings must be UL listed and so marked. Access to public elevators and escalators must not be blocked at any time. Utility panels, switchgear, fire hose cabinets, standpipes and fire extinguishers must remain visible and accessible at all times. Decorations may not block exit doors, fire extinguishing equipment, sprinklers, or emergency lighting systems. All decorating materials must be constructed of flameproof material or treated with an approved flame-proofing solution. Exhibitors may not use helium balloons, compressed gas, heaters, heating devices, or motorized vehicles without the express written consent of ASHP and the Walt Disney World Swan and Dolphin Hotel.

Children

Due to safety and health considerations, children under the age of 16 will not be admitted to the exhibit programme or educational sessions.

Limitation of Liability

The ASHP, the management of the Walt Disney World Swan and Dolphin Hotel, and the officers, directors, agents, employees, contractors and assigns of any of the aforesaid parties will not be responsible for any loss, injury or damage whatsoever or howsoever arising, which may occur to an exhibitor or to his agents, or employees, or to his contractors and its agents and employees, or to the property or wares of the exhibitor, arising from any cause whatsoever, in connection with this exhibit. Each exhibitor expressly releases ASHP and the above named parties from any and all claims for any such injury, loss or damage.

Liability of Exhibitor

If ASHP or the Walt Disney World Swan and Dolphin Hotel shall be subject to any claim, demand, liability, lawsuit, judgment (whether or not final) award of any type (whether or not final), for any damage or injury to person or property which arises directly or indirectly from the actions or failure to act of one or more exhibitors, their employees, agents, contractors or persons on or about the premises with a badge of the exhibitor, such exhibitor or exhibitors shall jointly and severally indemnify and hold harmless ASHP and the Walt Disney World Swan and Dolphin Hotel against any liability resulting from there, including without limitation, attorneys fees.

Insurance

Exhibitors must adequately insure their materials, goods, wares and exhibits against theft, damage, loss or injury of any kind and must do so at their own expense; ASHP and the Walt Disney World Swan and Dolphin Hotel are not responsible for any loss (howsoever caused) to any property of any exhibitor. Exhibitors are solely responsible for their own actions and all actions of their staff during the ASHP Summer Meeting.

Security

The ASHP will provide overall security guard service throughout the entire meeting including the official periods of exhibit installation and dismantling. The furnishing of such service is in no case to be understood or interpreted by exhibitors as guaranteeing them or insuring the content of their exhibit against loss or theft of any kind. For additional security services, please contact the Official Security Contractor for the meeting.

Use of ASHP Logo

Exhibitors will not use the ASHP logo, the name of ASHP nor in any manner associate any exhibit or any activity during the Summer Meeting with ASHP without the express written consent of its Director of Conference and Convention Planning.

New this year! Food and Beverage

Certain packaged foods and nonalcoholic beverages may be distributed by exhibitors from their exhibit space. The distribution of any food or beverages by exhibitors must be approved in advance by ASHP. Details are available in the service kit.

Exhibitors are advised of the policy approved by the ASHP House of Delegates regarding the consumption of alcoholic beverage:

"That alcohol is a drug and should be used with the respect and concern afforded to any drug; that pharmacists should extend their professional obligations and responsibilities to alcohol use by individuals and themselves; that pharmacists have an obligation to ensure that, if consumed, alcohol is used only responsibly; that pharmacists, by example in their personal conduct, should foster awareness of the nature of alcohol and responsible use of alcohol by those who choose to use alcohol; and that ASHP and its members continue to support and foster impaired-pharmacists programmes as a means of providing opportunities for such individuals to rehabilitate themselves".

Videotaping

Exhibitors are not permitted to audio or videotape sessions or exhibits during the meeting without written approval from the Exhibits Manager.

Other Rules and Regulations

All rights and privileges granted exhibitor are subject to and subordinated to a master lease between ASHP and the Walt Disney World Swan and Dolphin Hotel and its policies, rules, and regulations. This agreement provides a personal right to Exhibitor and creates no interest or estate in the Venetian or its equipment or facilities.

Exhibitor will comply with all applicable Federal, State and municipal statutes, ordinances, regulations, rules and requirements including without limitation laws applicable to patents, copyrights and trademarks and all rules and regulations of the Walt Disney World Swan and Dolphin Hotel.

Exhibitors will not discriminate against any person on account of race, creed, color, sex, religion, national origin or physical or mental disability.

Definitions: For purposes of these Rules and Regulations the following terms have the following meaning:

> "The Swan and Dolphin Hotel" means and includes the Walt Disney World Swan and Dolphin Hotel – Olrando which is engaged in business as the Swan and Dolphin Hotel, its respective directors, trustees, officers, employees, members and agents.
>
> "ASHP" includes and means the American Society of Health-System Pharmacists (ASHP), and its directors, officers, employees, agents, members, and contractors.

The Rules and Regulations of the Exhibit may be amended

by ASHP and such amendments are hereby made an integral part of and incorporated by reference into the Contract for Exhibit Space and shall be deemed to have the identical effect as if set forth in full in the Contract. All points not specifically covered are subject to the decision of the ASHP.

III

HOTEL FRONT OFFICE FUNCTION: A CASE STUDY OF ETHICS

Two weeks before her niece's wedding, Esther Barnes negotiated a room rate with the Panda Bear Inn. She received a reservation confirmation number for a double room for two people for two nights. When Esther and her husband arrived at the Panda Bear Inn, much to their dismay, they were told that their room was not available because the Inn had overbooked and they would be put up in a different hotel only five miles away.

They had been traveling most of the day and were very tired. Mrs. Barnes felt a little better when she was told that the Panda Bear Inn would pay for the room at the Lion's Gate Inn. Driving another five miles didn't seem too much of an inconvenience. However, when the front desk manager told her that the Panda Bear Inn would not host the Barnes' for the two nights at Lion's Gate, she became a little irritated. The manager further explained that Panda Bear Inn had openings for the second night and the Barnes' would have to return to the Inn for the second night. Since Esther wanted to retain the room rate she had negotiated, she agreed and the Barnes' left to stay at the Lion's Gate for their first night in town. After checking in at the Lions' Gate, they had to completely unpack and ready their clothes for the morning breakfast at her sister's house. The next day, they had to leave the family function and return to the Lion's Gate, repack their belongings, check out, and drive to the Panda Bear Inn. Once there, they again checked in, unpacked, and rushed to get ready for the late afternoon ceremony and the evening reception.

The next morning Esther and her husband felt like they spent more of their time packing and unpacking than they did visiting and celebrating with their relatives. During their trip home, Esther told her husband that their experience reminded her of getting bumped off a flight by an airline—but, in this case, they were not compensated for their inconvenience. She also questioned the legality of overbooking. She quipped, "What good is a confirmation number, when there is no guarantee of a room?" Esther decided to write a letter to the corporate headquarters of the Panda Bear Inn hotel chain.

Do no–shows and late cancellations justify overbooking? Do the operational advantages of overbooking outweigh the inconvenience to guests? Were the Barnes' treated properly? How would you feel if this happened to you? Consider an analogous situation. Imagine going to your hair stylist for a late Tuesday afternoon appointment. You expect to be there for two hours. You are very excited because that evening you are going to an important business function where you will meet many significant people in your field. However, when you arrive, you are told that Eva, your favourite hair stylist, is overbooked and the salon has arranged for you to have your hair done at the XYZ Salon, a half hour away. They explained to you that Tuesdays average three cancellations, so the salon always overbooks. On your Tuesday, however, there were no cancellations. Would you consider this acceptable behaviour on the part of the salon?

Case Commentary: Utilitarianism

The act utilitarian point of view on the Barnes's situation asks, "Was the greatest good achieved for the greatest number of people?" Possibly—the only ones inconvenienced were Mr. and Mrs. Barnes. The hotel owners certainly achieved their greatest good, at least in the short run. They made the most money possible by having sold all the rooms. However, allowing guests to think their rooms are guaranteed when they really are not, may have numerous harmful consequences for the hotel owners, both short term and long term. The corporation is using the guest to achieve the highest possible profit for that day, while paying less attention to the guest's needs and comfort.

What are the consequences if a hotel develops a reputation for consistently overbooking? What are the consequences if employees see overbooking as management's inconsiderate treatment of guests? Employees often take their cue from their supervisors. The housekeeper might decide that the bathroom looks "clean enough" for guests. The bellperson might decide to charge a guest for calling a taxi.

An act utilitarian considers all of the consequences of the action. There are also consequences to never overbooking: lost revenue for the hotel owners and empty rooms denied to travelers in need of lodging.

For act utilitarianism, deciding the morality of action involves a balancing act: you weigh the total benefits against the total harms likely to result from a specific act. You are ethically obligated to undertake the action that results in the greatest net benefit for all concerned.

In the case of overbooking, the many factors you must balance can make the calculation fairly complicated. If a hotel only overbooks by X percent of rooms, and the X percent overbooking rate very seldom results in any guest being "walked," the net harm is relatively small. Since the benefits of a full hotel are many, act utilitarianism may find this level of overbooking ethically acceptable, because the benefits outweigh the harms.

However, it is also a question of how injurious the harms are. If a guest denied a room because of overbooking is greatly harmed (forced to travel a great distance for alternative accommodations, or forced to accept inferior accommodations, etc.), then the weight may swing in the direction of making overbooking unethical.

Another factor that would affect the balance (and, hence, the morality of overbooking) is how much overbooking is practiced. If, instead of X percent of rooms being overbooked, three times X percent are overbooked, and this higher rate means that guests are frequently denied the rooms they reserved, then the amount of harm increases significantly. Thus, act utilitarianism may condone a certain level of overbooking but not higher levels.

It is all a matter of examining the amount of benefit and harm done, and choosing the course of action most likely to maximize the net benefit for all concerned. Rule utilitarianism applies the principle of "greatest good" to rules of conduct, not to individual acts. So the question is: can a rule allowing overbooking be morally justified? It is apparent that rules allowing frequent denial of reserved service would not produce "the greatest happiness for the greatest number," and thus they would be considered unethical. But it is quite possible that "mild" forms of overbooking, those that result in very few denials of reserved service and/or in small inconveniences, would be judged ethically acceptable.

Case Commentary: Kant's Categorical Imperative

Kant would view overbooking differently from the utilitarian perspective. He would be primarily concerned with the individual rights of the person denied what they were promised. If the hotel had overbooked because there had been a natural disaster in the area and they were trying to accommodate as many people as possible, Kant would maintain that this might be acceptable because of the motive behind the action. The overbooking was done out of a sense of duty to one's fellow man; it, therefore, may be the right thing to do. However from a Kantian ethical perspective, it would be much harder to justify overbooking as a routine business practice ensuring higher daily profits.

Consider the two formulations of Kant's categorical imperative that we have studied. First, we should act in a way that whatever rule we follow, we could will this to be a universal rule. Since a reservation is a promise to deliver a service (room, airline flight, etc.), denial of that service is breaking a promise. As with all forms of promising, Kant would condemn breaking the promise because breaking promises destroys the very basis of making a promise in the first place. It is self–contradictory to make a promise and break that promise; hence it is irrational and immoral. Thus, the first formulation of Kant's categorical imperative would condemn any overbooking that actually resulted in the denial of a promised service.

The second form of the categorical imperative stipulates that one must not use people for his or her own purposes. On the face of it, the practice of overbooking appears to do just that. Guests are used to ensure higher profits for the corporations without regard for the humanity or autonomy of those guests. Essentially, the guest has been "used" because he or she was, in effect, lied to when the reservation was made.

To illustrate this, consider the following situation. You arrive at your destination hotel after ten very long hours of traveling including a number of airplane changes, delays, bad weather, and lost luggage—only to find out that your room reservation was not honored. Imagine that you had guaranteed your late arrival and even called just a few hours earlier and were assured a room. Now imagine that you have to taxi to another location and you have the further inconvenience of informing the airline to deliver your lost luggage to this other destination. Would you feel used? Would you have been degraded from the status of a human being to that of a "thing" used for someone else's convenience?

There may be, however, another way that overbooking could be made compatible with Kantian ethics. If the guest or passenger is made aware, at the time the reservation is made, that a "reservation" does not actually guarantee a room or flight, only a very high likelihood of its availability, then no promise has been made. No deception would have occurred in the event of denial of "reserved" service. The guest or passenger would not have been "used" because he or she was aware in advance that there is at least a slight possibility of denial of service. He or she would then be able to rationally make a decision about what to do, and no deception or denial of humanity has occurred.

These appear to be the only circumstances where Kant would find overbooking to be morally acceptable. This is an example of a practice where Kantian ethics is much stricter than utilitarian ethics, which may find overbooking ethically acceptable in a larger number of circumstances than would Kant.

Case Commentary: The Ethic of Justice

Justice ethics states that we should treat each other fairly and asks us to look at the situation from behind the veil of ignorance. Imagine that you do not know if you were to be the front desk manager (who earns a bonus based on profit and daily occupancy rates) or if you were to be the weary traveler who discovers that the "guaranteed" room reservation was, in fact, not guaranteed. If everyone involved in making the decision were both rational and interested in their own well being, many of the more permissive forms of overbooking would not be tolerated. A rational person would set up rules protecting the interests of the traveler, since he or she may end up being that traveler. Even if mild forms of overbooking were to be allowed, a justice ethic would place strong and effective restrictions on the practice.

Compensatory justice would also dictate that the wronged guest must be compensated for the loss and inconvenience. Some suggest that a guest might expect a free night at a nearby hotel of the same or better quality, a free phone call to notify friends or family of the hotel change, and a free upgrade on a future visit. Is this enough compensation for the traveler? Is this fair to the traveler? What if the person never expects to be in the area again? What good would the future upgrade do? In considering what is fair, you must ask questions such as: what has the hotel lost and what has the guest lost? What is the compensation costing the hotel? What is the denial of a room costing the potential guest?

Case Commentary: Aristotle and the Ethics of Virtue

Virtue ethics would view the hotel as a human community and ask how well does the hotel contribute to the development of the character traits of its employees? The traits or virtues include honesty, integrity, tolerance, fairness, and cooperation. Overbooking raises concerns about how well a hotel fosters honesty, integrity, and fairness if it does not keep its word to its guests. Any enterprise that engages in overbooking needs to be sure that this practice is honest and open and it does not promote an ethic of deception or irresponsibility in its employees. Virtue ethics requires businesses to foster values that relate to the way it interacts with its community. A business has to display a solid ethical culture in order to be respected by its community.

IV

GENERAL CONDITIONS TO THE SERVICED RENTAL AGREEMENT IN THE FRENCH HOTELS: A MODEL

In addition to the provisions overleaf, the Serviced Rental Agreement is governed by articles 1714 to 1762 of the French civil Code and the General Conditions below. In no event shall it fall within the scope law n°89-462 dated 6 July 1989 (serviced rentals, rentals of secondary homes, rentals as condition of employment contract), or law n°48-1360 dated 1 September 1948.

I. Duration - Termination

The duration of the contract is freely determined by the parties.

II. Rent

The amount of the rent is freely determined between the

Parties. For practical purposes, it is agreed that the amount of the rent can be paid by the Lessee either on an Internet website owned by TRIPINKIT SARL or directly to the Lessor.

III. Inventory of Fixtures

An inventory of fixtures can be appended to this agreement. In such a case, the inventory shall be filled out by both parties and it shall be delivered either to the Lessee with the keys or in the hotel. In the absence of inventory, and pursuant to article 1731 of the French civil Code, premises shall be deemed as in suitable conditions.

Upon termination of this agreement, a check out inventory can be jointly established by the parties. Such check out inventory shall be subject to a 2 days prior notice and shall occur within business hours.

IV. Obligations of the Lessee

The Lessee shall:

1. Have paid the amount of the rent to TRIPINKIT - YellowStay.
2. Make normal use of the premises and related facilities, in accordance with the residential use set out in the Serviced Rental Agreement.
3. Be liable for any deterioration and/or loss that may occur in the premises during the term of this agreement, except if such deteriorations have been caused by Force Majeure, by the Lessor or by any third party provided that the Lessee did not allow such party to enter into the premises.
4. Immediately inform the Lessor of any damage or deterioration that may occur in the premises, even if the said damage or deterioration is not apparent.
5. Not transform the premises or its appliance/ installations without prior written approval of

the Lessor. In case of non compliance by the Lessee with this obligation, the Lessor shall be entitled to request that the premises and installations be returned to their initial state. All necessary work shall be carried out by the Lessee or the Lessor, at Lessor's option. All related costs shall be borne by the Lessee.

6. Allow any renovation work to be carried out in the communal or private parts of the premises, as well as any general repair required. Provisions of articles 1724 al 2 and 3 shall apply to any renovation work.
7. Comply with the premises rules and regulations, as displayed in the premises communal areas.
8. Comply and immediately carry out any request or instruction of the Lessor made pursuant to the decisions of co-owners general meeting or pursuant to provisions of the premises rules and regulations.
9. Personally occupy the premises; not transfer the Serviced Rental Agreement to any person without Lessor's prior written approval. In the event of transfer of the Serviced Rental Agreement without Lessor's prior approval as aforementioned, the transferee shall have no right over the premises or vis à vis the Lessor.
10. In the case of the sale of the premises, allow visits of the premises, two hours a day within business hours.
11. In no event move the furniture outside the premises.
12. Not to leave the premises without having satisfied all its obligations pursuant to the Serviced Rental Agreement and these General Conditions.
13. Give back the keys of the premises to the Lessor prior to departure from the premises and provide a forwarding address.

V. Obligations of the Lessor

The Lessor shall:

1. Hand over the premises and its installations in good conditions.
2. Procure that the Lessee benefit from a normal occupancy right without prejudice of the provisions of article 1721 of the French civil Code.
3. Maintain the premises in suitable condition for the purposes of the Serviced Rental Agreement.
4. Provide the Lessee with the appropriate receipt of the rent upon Lessee's request.
5. Provide the premises as described on its commercial vitrine.

VI. Termination

The Serviced Rental Agreement can be terminated:

- By the Lessee: only at the end of the term.
- By the Lessor: upon a reasonable prior notice to the Lessee.

In addition, the Serviced Rental Agreement shall be immediately terminated by the Lessor in the event that the Lessee defaults in any of its obligations pursuant to the Serviced Rental Agreement or these General Conditions.

In case of termination, for any reason whatsoever, the Lessee shall immediately leave the premises. Should the Lessee refuse to comply with this obligation to leave the premises, the Lessee shall be liable to pay to the Lessor, for each day beyond the date at which the Lessee should have left the premises, an amount corresponding to twice the daily rent amount, without prejudice of the Lessor's right to claim for additional damages or indemnification before French Courts.

VII. Indulgence

In no event any indulgence of the Lessor in respect of any infringement to the provisions of the Serviced Rental Agreement or these General Conditions shall be considered as an acceptance or a modification of said Serviced Rental Agreement or General Conditions whatever the frequency and duration of such infringement.

VIII. Miscellaneous

The Serviced Rental Agreement and these General Conditions shall be governed by French law. For the purposes of the Serviced Rental Agreement and these General Conditions the parties decide to elect as their domicile, for the Lessor: its registered office, and for the Lessee: in the premises rent to him.

IX. Cancellation

Cancellations: In the event of cancellation from the lessee:

- Given at least 14 days in advance, monies paid will be refunded in full minus 60 euros for administration fees.
- For cancellations between 14 days and 4 days notice, NO monies will be returned unless the accommodation is re-let (the deposit will be kept).
- For cancellations with less than 4 days notice or NO SHOW, 50 per cent of the total price will be charged to the lessee.
- Once arrived in the hotel, the lessee has 12 hours to refuse the premises by contacting the lessor with suffisiants grounds. If the lessor is not contacted, the "NO SHOW" case will be applyed.

If the accommodation is re-let, a commercial gesture is possible from the lessor, please contact it by e-mail/phone.You can normally acquire insurance against this.

Cancellations: In the event of cancellation from the lessor

If, for any phisical reasons (storm, fire, technicals problems with electricity/water), the premises could not be delivered in time, the lessor must contact the lessee to find an arrangement/an alternative accomodation. ANY cancellation must be established on a written document in two copies, one for each parties.

X. Extras

The lessee accepts to be charged of ANY extras used in the premises as phone communications and extra movies ordered on-line. The lessor will inform the lesse of these extra charges.

V

COUNTRY OF WAYNE RULES AND REGULATIONS: A CASE STUDY

Part 1: General

A. Purpose

The purpose of these Rules and Regulations are:

- To establish the procedures for the collection of the Wayne County Hotel Room Rental Excise Tax by the Operators in the market area of Hotels, Motels, Inns, Guest Houses and Bed and Breakfast or any Lodging facility that are available to provide overnight lodging or use of the facility space for consideration to persons seeking temporary accommodation located in Wayne County.
- To establish the procedures for the remittance of the Wayne County Hotel Room Rental Excise Tax by the Operators to the Wayne County Treasurer's Office.

— To establish the official reporting procedures and forms to be utilized by the operators, and other relevant Rules and Regulations concerning the collection of the Wayne County Hotel Room Rental Excise Tax.

B. Objectives

These Rules and Regulations are designed to establish a uniform practice and procedure for the imposition and collection of the Wayne County Hotel Room Rental Excise Tax. The Rules and Regulations are intended to guide and assist Operators to determine which Patrons are subject to the Wayne County Hotel Room Rental Excise Tax and the amount due by each Patron. The Rules and Regulations also estab1ish the official forms for the reporting and remittance of the Wayne County Hotel Room Rental Excise Tax to the Treasurer's Office, as well as general collection procedures.

C. Definitions

As used hereinafter, those terms, which are defined in Section 3 of Ordinance Number 61405 ("Ordinance"), shall have the identical meaning for the purpose of these Rules and Regulations, and are incorporated herein by reference.

Part II: Rules and Regulations

A. Imposition of Tax

1. Rate of Tax: The Wayne County Hotel Room Rental Excise Tax is imposed at the rate of three percent (3%) on any Transaction. 2. Collection of Tax by the Operator: The Wayne County Hotel Room Rental Excise Tax shall be collected by the Operator of each lodging facility, at the time of the Transaction from each Patron who pays the Consideration of the Transaction.

3. Effective Date: The Wayne County Hotel Roam Rental Excise Tax shall be applicable to all Transactions specified in Part II. A. 1. and Part II. A. 2., above which occur on and after August 1, 2005.

B. Registration

Prior to July 29, 2005,or within fifteen days after commencing business, whichever is later, each Operator of any Lodging facility shall register with the Wayne County Treasurer's Office by completing the application form provided by the Treasurer, a copy of which is attached as Form 1. The Operator of the Lodging facility shall obtain from the Treasurer a permanent Certificate of Authorization evidencing the Operator's authority to collect the Wayne County Hotel Room Rental Excise Tax, and the certificate shall at all times be posted in a conspicuous place on the premises of the Lodging facility.

C. Items Subject to Tax

The Occupancy of any Room, for Consideration, is subject to the Wayne County Hotel Room Rental Excise Tax. Exclusion for meals included in the rental fee paid by a patron is allowed.

D. Permament Residetns

1. General: The Wayne County Hotel Room Rental Excise Tax shall be imposed for Occupancy by Transients and not for Permanent Residents. after a Patron has:

— Occupied a room for thirty (30) consecutive days, the Patron is no longer a "transient" as defined in the Ordinance. The Patron's status as a "permanent resident" becomes effective at the expiration of the thirtieth consecutive day of Occupancy at the same lodging facility and continues thereafter so long as the Patron's Occupancy remains continuous and uninterrupted at the same lodging facility.

2. Procedure for Credits: Upon a Patron obtaining Permanent Resident status the Operator shall give the Patron a refund or credit for the thirty (30) days preceding the Patron's achieving Permanent Resident status.

— The Operator is entitled to a credit for the Operator's refund or credit to the Patron. The Operator's credit shall be noted on the next quarterly return filed by the Operator.

3. Guidelines for Implementation: A rental period, for the purpose of this subsection, is a period of time, (for example, a day, week, month or the like), during which, under and subject to the terms of a legally enforceable contract, a Patron has a continuous right to occupy a room or rooms in a Lodging facility and is legally bound to pay Consideration. (In the absence of evidence to the contrary, it is presumed that a rental period runs from the date of first occupancy or first payment of Consideration to the date on which a subsequent payment or Consideration is due.) A mere statement of intention to occupy or to permit occupancy, on the part of a Patron or Operator, or both, does not create a rental period unless the period in question is the subject of a legally enforceable contract.

— The occupancy or right of occupancy must be for thirty (30) consecutive days. A Patron who merely has the right to use a room or rooms on intermittent days of a week or month cannot become a "Permanent Resident" even though the Patron cumulatively occupies a room for more than any thirty (30) day period.

— The status of Permanent Residents only continues so long as the Occupancy or right of Occupancy continues uninterrupted. A Permanent Resident who breaks the consecutive and continuing Occupancy loses the status as a Permanent Resident and with respect to the Patron's next occupancy, the Patron does not resume the status of a permanent Resident unless and until the Patron again completes thirty (30) consecutive days of Occupancy. A transfer from one Lodging facility to another, even though both Lodging facilities are owned and/or operated by the same Operator, is a break in Occupancy. A mere change of rooms within the same Lodging facility is not a break in Occupancy, for the purpose of permanent resident exemption.

E. Exemptions

A Permanent Resident, as that term is defined in the Ordinance, is exempt from the Wayne County Hotel Room Rental Excise Tax in accordance with these Rules and Regulations. Other persons may also be exempt from the tax for other legal reasons, including the same exclusions that apply to Commonwealth Occupancy.

F. Records of Exempt Occupancies

The Operator shall maintain records to support and identify all exempt occupancies. The records shall include a form to be completed and signed by the exempt person. Form 3 attached. The Operator shall also sign and provide to the Treasurer a quarterly statement itemizing all exemptions claimed on a form provided by the Treasurer. Form 4 attached.

G. Reports, Returns, Payments, and Collecton of Tax

1. Collections from Patron: The Operator shall collect the Wayne County Hotel Room Rental Excise Tax imposed by the Ordinance from the Patron of the Room, and remit the same to the Treasurer as provided herein. The Operator shall be liable to Wayne County, as agent thereof, for the payment of the Wayne County Hotel Room Rental Excise Tax as provided in the Ordinance.

2. Monthly Return by Operator: On or before the twenty-fifth (25th) day of the calendar month after the close of each calendar quarter, the Operator shall submit to the Treasurer a return, that shall contain the previous calendar quarter's information, together with the remittance of the Wayne County Hotel Room Rental Excise Tax due by check made

payable to the "Wayne County Treasurer". The return shall include the amount of the Wayne County Hotel Room Rental Excise Tax collected by the Operator and any other information as the Treasurer may require from time to time. Form 2 attached.

3. Forms: Every report and return shall be made upon the official forms furnished by the Treasurer. The Treasurer reserves the right to, from time to time, amend and/or modify any form. The Treasurer also reserves the right to develop any and all forms to effectuate and implement the Ordinance or these Rules and Regulations. A copy of the current official forms is made part hereof and is attached hereto and identified as—Form 1, Form 2, Form 3, Form 4.

4. Interest for Late Returns: If any amount of tax due is not remitted by the due date, interest at the rate of nine (9.0) percent per year or three-quarters (.75) percent per month shall be added for each month or fraction thereof during which any of the Wayne County Hotel Room Rental Excise Tax shall remain unpaid or not properly remitted in accordance with these Rules and Regulations.

5. Late Filing Fee: If any return is filed after the due date, a late filing fee of $50.00 will be due and payable with the return.

H. Failure to Collectand Report Tax, Determination of Tax by the Treasurer, Failure to Remit Tax

1. Collection and Report: If any Operator shall fail to register with the Treasurer or shall fail or refuse to collect the Wayne County Hotel Room Rental Excise Tax under these Rules and Regulations, or fails or refuses to produce any report or form required by these Rules and Regulations, the Treasurer shall proceed in such manner as the Treasurer shall deem proper to obtain facts and information on which to base the estimate of the Wayne County Hotel Room Rental Excise Tax due, together with any interest, costs and attorney's fees. As soon as the Treasurer has procured the

facts and information as may be obtained, the Treasurer shall determine the amount of the Wayne County Hotel Room Rental Excise Tax due and payable by the Operator, together with any interest, costs and attorney's fees. ("Determination"). The Treasurer shall give notice of the Determination by personal service or by United States mail, postage prepaid, addressed to the operator at the Operator's last known place of business. The Operator may within ten (10) days after the service of the Determination make application in writing to the Treasurer for a hearing on the amount assessed in the Determination. If the Operator does not make such application within the time prescribed, the amount due under the Determination shall become final and conclusive and immediately become due and payable. If the Operator does provide such application, the Treasurer shall give no less than five (5) days prior written notice to the Operator of a hearing to show cause why the Determination is improper. At such hearing, the Operator may appear and offer evidence why the Treasurer determination is improper. At the conclusion of the hearing, the Chief Clerk shall ascertain the proper Pike County Hotel Room Rental Excise Tax due, together with any interest, costs and attorney's fees and shall provide written notice to the-Operator of the total amount due ("Assessment"). The assessment shall be payable within thirty (30) days unless an appeal is taken pursuant to these Rules and Regulations.

2. Failure to Remit: If an Operator fails to timely remit the Wayne County Hotel Room Rental Excise Tax collected by the Operator to the Treasurer, the Treasurer shall provide at least ten (10) day-s written notice to the Operator of the tax, interest, late filing fee, costs and attorney's fees to be assessed on untimely remittance. If the operator fails to remit the collected Wayne County Hotel Room Rental Excise Tax, together with any interest, late filing fee, costs and attorney's fees within ten (10) days from date of such notice, Treasurer County or its designee shall proceed with the filing of any and all claims and/or actions against the Operator

in the Court of Common Pleas of Wayne County. Except as otherwise provided by the Ordinance or these Rules and Regulations, the Operator shall be considered by the Treasurer to perform the duty of collection of the Wayne County Hotel Rom Rental Excise Tax under the same fiduciary obligation as placed on local tax collectors under the Pennsylvania Local Tax Collection Law.

I. Appeal

Any Operator aggrieved by a decision of the Treasurer with respect to the amount due for the Wayne County Hotel Room Rental Excise Tax, Interest, late filing fee, costs and attorney's fees may appeal the decision of the Treasurer to the Court of Common Pleas of Wayne County, pursuant to the applicable rules of the Pennsylvania Rules of Civil Procedure. The Treasurer reserves the right to waive such interest, late filing fee, costs, or attorney's fees based upon good cause shown.

J. Records

It is presumed that all Rooms are subject to the Wayne County Hotel Room Rental Excise Tax until accurate records of the Operator establish contrary. The burden of proving that the Transaction is not taxable is upon the Operator and the Operator must demonstrate the same through accurate records. In any case where an Operator fails to maintain adequate records as required under these Rules and Regulations, any Room for which there is not adequate records shall be deemed to be occupied for the entire period for which the supporting records are lacking. It shall be the duty of every Operator liable for the collection of the Wayne County Hotel Room Rental Excise Tax to keep and preserve for a period of three (3) years all records as may be necessary to determine the amount Of such tax for which the Operator was liable to collect and pay to Wayne County. The records shall be maintained at the place of business where the subject rooms were rented. The records shall include but are not limited to folios, lease agreements; general ledgers; night auditor and housekeeper reports; traffic summaries; source of business reports; and any other documents that support room revenue and exemptions. The records shall be filed in a manner that allows ready access by the Treasurer, or their authorized agents, who shall have the right to inspect the records during regular business hours of the Operator and to perform an audit thereon. In all instances where an Operator claims an exemption to the Ordinance pursuant to Rules and Regulations (Section E), the Operator shall retain copies of Form 3 of the Patron or other records indicating the exempt Patron's identifying information.

K. Refunds

Whenever the amount of the Wayne County Hotel Room Rental Excise Tax, interest, costs or attorney's fees has been overpaid; paid more than once, or erroneously collected or received by the Treasurer under the Ordinance, the overpayment may be refunded to the Operator provided that a verified written claim is filed by the Operator with the Treasurer within three (3) years of the date of payment stating the specific grounds upon which the claim is founded. The Operator must either return the refunded payment to the Patron or credit such amount to the Patron's account. If the Patron's whereabouts are unknown or unascertainable after reasonable investigation, such refund shall be resubmitted by the Operator to the Treasurer and shall be subject to the applicable escheat laws and statutes.

L. Actions to Collect

Any Wayne County Hotel Room Rental Excise Tax collected by an Operator that has not been paid to the Treasurer shall be deemed a debt owed by the Operator to Wayne County. Any Patron or Operator owing monies to Wayne County pursuant to the provisions of the Ordinance and these Rules and Regulations shall be liable to Wayne County for the same. Any action to collect brought under the Ordinance or these Rules and Regulations shall be brought by Wayne County or Wayne County's designee, Any actions brought under the Ordinance or these Rules and Regulations by Wayne County's designee shall include the Wayne County Hotel Room Rental Excise Tax, any interest due under the Rules and Regulations, and any costs and attorney's fees associated with the collection thereof.

M. Right to Privacy

All reports, returns, and forms submitted to the Treasurer are subject to public disclosure under the Pennsylvania Right to Know Law. The Treasurer shall not disclose any confidential information, which is otherwise protected by law.

N. Severability of Provisions

In the event any provision, section, sentence, clause or part of these Rules and Regulations shall be held to be invalid; such invalidity shall not affect or impair any remaining provision, section, sentence, clause, or part of these Rules and Regulations, it being the intent of the Treasurer that the remainder of these Rules and Regulations shall remain in full force and effective.

O. Amendments

The Treasurer reserves the right to, from time to time, without advance notice, amend and/or supplement these Rules and Regulations as it pertains to the collection and enforcement of the Wayne County Hotel Room Rental Excise Tax. Amendments and/or supplements to the Rules and Regulations shall be made available to the Operators.

VI

RENTAL LONDON: A UK MODEL

London Rentals

Accommodation and Transport are the primary facilities that shine out in the hire business at London. However the terms and conditions are different for the inhabitants and the non-aboriginals. The Rental London real estate agencies provide friendly assistance to both the natives and the immigrants in facilitating the lease transactions.

Accomodation on Lease

Acquiring an accommodation in a city like London is of over 7.5 million of population isn't difficult at all. The Lease agencies work to support the natives, tourists and immigrants in acquiring quality accommodation as per the financial status and the requirements. However there are terms and conditions stated by law that have to be followed in order to make the lease transactions legal. Awareness of these rules and regulations protect the tenants and landlords from legal controversies. The information below states the criteria of getting a house on lease.

Regulations for Availing House on Rental London

A Tenancy agreement has to be signed by both the tenant and the landlord. The Tenancy Agreement should not conflict with the Law. Both landlord and tenants share the rights and responsibilities given by the law.

The Tenancy Agreement is categorized into two:

1. Drafted Agreement: It comprises of what is written in the agreement and also what is settled between the landlord and the tenant orally. In England most of the tenants have a right to drafted lease agreement. The specimen of the written agreement are supplied by some solicitors and real estate agents
2. Inferential Agreement: It comprises of those rights, which are established by Law, Custom and Practice.

The Drafted Agreement should include the following:

(1) Names and addresses of both the landlord and the tenant.

(2) The date when Tenancy began

(3) Duration of the tenancy stating the date when it runs out

(4) The amount and the procedure of the payment of the rent detailing the time and the structure.

(5) Any expenses the landlord would want t include for e.g. Fuel.

(6) Services if any provided by the landlord

(7) The notice period of ending the tenancy which depends upon the type of tenancy for which there are rules in Law.

For more information one can log on to www.adviceguide.org.uk

The Inferential agreement includes clauses such as:

(a) Basic repairs should be carried out by the landlord

(b) The installation for the water supply, gas, electricity, sanitation, space heating and heating water in good working order should be ensured.

(c) The right to have a peaceful accommodation without any nuisance from the landlord.

(d) The tenant should ensure that he would take good care of the accommodation.

A tenancy Agreement is a form of a Consumer Contract and must be written in simple language so that it does not become unfavourable to any. A tenant has rights in Law to avail documents and information such as:

(i) A rent book or an allied document in case of a short stay which is not fixed. The landord becomes liable for committing an offence if its not granted.

(ii) A document stating the full name and addresses of the landlord .A request can be made to the agent in case of its unavailability who shall provide them within 21 days after which he shall become liable for an offence.

Advisers at The Citizens Advice Bureau should be consulted in obtaining documents of any kind from the landlord. Changes can be brought in the agreement with the consent of both the tenant and the landlord. The amendment can either be made in the same drafted agreement or a new agreement can be made.

In order to avail a house on hire there are various websites that can be logged on, which provide the advertisements stating the details such as rental price, facilities, atmosphere, location, payment procedures etc. Some of them are:

(a) www.londonettes.co.uk: This website advertises Short term rentals in London for business and holiday travelers.
(b) www.homerentalconnections.com: It advertises privately owned appartments for the purposes of vacation and business.
(c) www.woogo.com: It states 70% off serviced premier apartments for short or long stay.
(d) www.londonpropertyforrent.com: It provides the list of houses on rent.
(e) www.appartments-hotels.com: It lists the apartments and hotels for the tourists.

Transporatation on Lease

The rules of transportation in the U.K ARE ALMOST THE SAME FOR the aboriginals, foreign nationals, tourists, immigrants etc, but include some reservations for the transportation on hire such as:

(1) Foreign Nationals who wish to hire a car in the U.K are required to have a passport and a driving license.
(2) The seat belts are compulsory in the front and must be worn in the hired car.
(3) Drinking while driving is prohibited while driving

hired cars – currently the blood alcohol is at 35mg/100mg

(4) The Road Laws such as speed limits, parking zones, road signs and markings should be considered. The speed limit observed by the rental cars in The U.K is 112kph/70mph; in the urban areas it is 48 kph/30mph; in major roads it is 65kph/40mph; in the residential area it is 35kph/25mph.

The first thing to realise is that the U.K motorists drive rental cars on the left.

The website www.car-rental-hire.co.uk provides a list of the cars that can be hired for all purposes like holiday, airport pick ups, wedding etc

The cars available on this address are:

(a) Vans: Ford Escort Fiat Scudo, Transit Van, Ford Transit Hi-roof van
(b) Minibuses
(c) Chauffeur drive hire cars
(d) Cars for self drive

Car on lease for airport collection includes a procedure that has to be followed in order to avail hospitality at the time when one boards off the plane. The procedure is as follows:

1. A registration has to be made in airport office dealing in the hire business.
2. After which rental documents containing the pick and drop procedure is provided in a particular period of time

In case a car has to be bought on lease for driving overseas a different booking criteria has to be followed.

VII

MODEL STUDY: THE HOTEL KEEPERS ACT (C.C.S.M. C. H150), MANITOBA

HER MAJESTY, by and with the advice and consent of the Legislative Assembly of Manitoba, enacts as follows:

Definitions

1. In this Act,

"hotel" includes an inn, tavern, public house or other place of refreshment; (« hôtel ») and "hotel keeper" includes the keeper of a hotel. (« hôtelier »)

Lien for board and lodging

2. Any hotel keeper, or boarding house keeper, or lodging house keeper, may detain in his hotel or house, before they have been removed thereout but not afterwards, the trunks, valises, and personal effects, including clothing, of any person who may be indebted to him for an amount incurred by the person while a guest of the hotel or boarding house or lodging house.

Responsibility for goods detained

3. Every hotel keeper, boarding house keeper, and lodging house keeper, shall keep in his possession, and is responsible for, any trunks and valises and their contents and any personal effects detained by him for the full period of the detention, unless they are sooner released.

Right to sell goods detained

4. Where, at the expiry of the period of detention hereinafter mentioned, the amount for which the trunks, valises, or personal effects, have been detained has not been paid, the keeper of the hotel, boarding house, or lodging house, upon complying with this Act, may sell them or any part thereof by public auction.

Power to break open trunks, etc.

5. After the expiration of the period of one month, if the amount aforesaid has not been paid, the keeper of the hotel, boarding house, or lodging house may, in the presence of a justice of the peace, force or break any locks or fastenings on any trunk, box, valise, or other article detained by him as aforesaid for the purpose of ascertaining and inspecting the contents thereof.

Notice of sale to be given

6(1) At least one month before the day fixed for the sale the hotel keeper, boarding house keeper, or lodging house keeper, shall mail in a registered package a notice of the intended sale, addressed to the person so indebted to him, directed to the person's last known address.

Contents of notice

6(2) The notice shall contain

(a) a general description of the trunks, valises, personal property or effects, to be sold, and the date and place of the proposed sale;

(b) an itemized statement of the charges of the hotel keeper, boarding house keeper, or lodging house keeper, showing the sum due at the time of the notice;

(c) a demand that the amount of the charges, as stated in the notice, shall be paid on or before the day of sale; and

(d) a statement that if the amount of the charges, as stated in the notice, is not paid on or before the day of sale, the property will be sold by public auction at the time and place specified.

Application of proceeds of sale and proceeds

6(3) After the sale the keeper of the hotel, boarding house, or lodging house may apply the proceeds thereof in payment of the amount due to him and the reasonable cost of advertising and ofthe auctioneer; and he shall pay over the surplus, if any, to the person entitled thereto on application being made by him therefor; and if application therefor is not forthwith made he shall immediately pay it to the Registrar of the Court of Queen's Bench.

Duty of Registrar

6(4) The Registrar shall keep the amount for that person for one year, after which time, if the person does not appear or claim the amount so kept, it shall be paid over to the Minister of Finance and form part of the Consolidated Fund.

Liability of hotel keeper for the property of his guests

7. No hotel keeper is liable to make good to any guest of the hotel any loss or injury to goods or property brought to his hotel except

(a) where the goods or property are stolen, lost, or injured, through the fault or neglect of the hotel keeper or any servant in his employ; or

(b) subject to subsection 8(1), where the goods or property are deposited expressly for safe custody with the hotel keeper.

Conditions whereby deposit made

8(1) Where a deposit is made, as mentioned in clause 7(b), the hotel keeper may, if he thinks fit require, as a condition of his liability, that the goods or property be deposited in a box or receptacle fastened and sealed by the person depositing it.

Receipt for property deposited

8(2) Any person so depositing money, jewellery, documents or other valuables of a similar nature, as provided in section 7, shall demand and receive from the keeper of the hotel, boarding house, or lodging house, a receipt therefor; and before he is entitled to receive the articles to which the receipt refers from the hotel keeper, the person shall surrender the receipt given by the hotel keeper at the time the deposit was made.

Refusal of hotel keeper to receive valuables

8(3) Where a hotel keeper refuses to receive for safe keeping, as before mentioned, money, jewellery, documents or valuables of a similar nature, the property of his guest, or where any such guest, through any default of the hotel keeper, is unable to deposit any such money, jewellery, documents or other valuables of a similar nature, as aforesaid, the hotel keeper is not entitled to the benefit of this Act in respect of the money, jewellery, documents or other valuables, unless he can show that his hotel was not equipped with a proper safe or vault and he had so informed the guest at the time of refusing to receive the property.

Responsibilities of hotel keepers, etc., in respect of personal effects

9(1) Notwithstanding anything in this Act no hotel keeper, boarding house keeper, or lodging house keeper, is responsible for any trunks or their contents, or any parcels or personal effects of any kind, left by guests, boarders, or lodgers in their rooms, if there are proper locks and keys for the doors of those rooms, unless the rooms are locked and the keys thereof left at the office.

Where checking room provided

9(2) Where any such hotel keeper, boarding house keeper, or lodging house keeper has provided a suitable parcel or checking room or office in his premises, he is not responsible or liable for the loss of any chattels, personal effects, or property of any kind, left in the hotel, boarding house, or lodging house, unless they are brought to the checking room or office and a check therefor demanded by the owner or person in charge of the property.

Undesirable persons may be ejected

10. A hotel keeper or his representative may require any person, not a guest of the hotel, whom he deems undesirable, to leave the hotel; and if the person fails to leave, may eject him from the hotel premises.

Exemptions under Executions Act not to apply

11. The exemptions provided for in *The Executions Act* or *The Judgments Act* do not apply to a judgment obtained or executed, or certificate issued thereon, for any amount due to a hotel keeper, boarding house keeper, or lodging house keeper, solely for board and lodging.

VIII

HOTEL REWARD PROGRAMMES - CHOICE PRIVILEGES - RULES AND REGULATIONS

Choice Hotels International, Inc. ("Choice") provides these Rules and Regulations for the *Choice Privileges®* Rewards Programme ("Programme"). Choice may amend these Rules and Regulations at any time. For Canadian residents, the Programme is owned by Choice Hotels Canada, Inc. and administered by Choice.

General Programme Information

1. Choice offers programme membership to individuals 18 years or older only and not to corporations or other entities. You may establish and maintain only one Member account.
2. After reviewing your completed Member application, Choice will provide you with a Member number. When you receive your Member number, Choice will inform you when you are eligible to receive Hotel Benefits and earn Points. Choice will not apply Points or airline rewards or provide you with Hotel Benefits before processing your application and activating your Member number.

3. You must maintain a U.S. or Canadian address (including U.S. territories) to be a Member, receive hotel benefits designated below ("Hotel Benefits"), earn and redeem Points ("Points"), and receive Programme statements.
4. You earn Points or airline rewards for individual travel on the following qualifying standard rate plans (SRPs). They are: Rack, Corporate (SCR, CORP, LCORP), VIP (SPC), Net Preferred (SNP), Government/Military (SGM, GOVT), 50+ Mature Traveler (SSC), Travelers' Discount (STD), AAA/CAA (S3A, AAA, LAAA), Inn-to-Inn (SII), Small Organisation Savings/Significant Savings (SSO), Sixty Plus Rate (SSV), Sports Rate (LSPRT), CPSA (LR7), negotiated rates (N), and select local rate plans.

Programme Communications/Reservations

1. As a *Choice Privileges* member you will receive e-mail and printed newsletters describing special programme news, promotions and benefits.
2. As a Member, you may make reservations at the Choice Business (corporate) Rate (if available) or at other rates through the Program's toll-free express reservation line ("Programme Line"), your travel agent, or the Programme website (choiceprivileges.com).
3. You may use the Programme Line in the U.S., Caribbean and Canada only.
4. The Choice Business Rate cannot be combined with any other discount or promotional offers.

Earning Points

1. As a Member, you are the only person who may earn Points for your account.

2. A "stay" is defined as any number of consecutive nights at one hotel regardless of check-ins or check-outs.
3. You earn Points for up to two rooms per night. Both rooms must be in your name and include your member number. You must stay in one of the rooms and pay for both rooms. You only receive any applicable bonus points on one room. Elite members only earn Elite status on one room per stay.
4. If your individual hotel bill is billed directly to a company and you are responsible for authorization of settlement at check-out, your stay is eligible for *Choice Privileges* points. However, group master-billing arrangements where charges for multiple rooms are placed on one hotel bill and billed to a company or common address or settled at check-out by one individual are not eligible.
5. If both you and another Member share a room, Choice will credit Points to the Member reserving and staying in the room.
6. You do not earn Points for complimentary rooms, rooms paid for by third parties as part of a convention or meeting, or rooms booked through a travel agent as a part of wholesale packages or series tours.
7. You earn 10 Points for each whole U.S. dollar that you pay in full in room revenue when paying qualifying rates, excluding taxes, restaurant or other incidental charges at Comfort Inn, Comfort Suites, Quality, Sleep Inn, Clarion, Cambria Suites and MainStay Suites hotels in the U.S., Canada, Caribbean and Mexico and at Econo Lodge® and Rodeway Inn® hotels throughout Canada. Econo Lodge and Rodeway Inn properties in the U.S.

participate in the EA$Y CHOICE® rewards programme.

8. Allow 72 hours after checking out of the hotel for Points to post to your account.
9. *Choice Privileges* Points expire on December 31, two years after the year in which they were deposited into your account unless forfeited or canceled earlier due to membership inactivity or otherwise in accordance to these rules and regulations.
10. You may not earn Points and airline rewards for the same stay. You must choose either Points or airline rewards and notify the hotel of your preference upon check-in.
11. Allow 3 weeks after your Enterprise Rent-A-Car transaction is complete for Points to post to your account.

Earning Airline Rewards

1. You must be a member of a participating frequent flyer programme and abide by that program's rules and regulations to earn airline rewards.
2. You must provide your frequent flyer number at check-in. Guest name must match frequent flyer membership name to earn airline rewards.
3. You may earn 250 miles with Aeroplan®, Alaska Airlines Mileage Plan, the American Airlines AAdvantage® programme, Continental Airlines OnePass®, Delta SkyMiles®, Frecuenta by Mexicana, Northwest Airlines® WorldPerks®, United Mileage Plus® or US Airways® Dividend Miles® or receive 0.5 Southwest Airlines Rapid Rewards® credits per stay at any Comfort Inn, Comfort Suites, Quality, Sleep Inn, Clarion,

Cambria Suites or MainStay Suites hotel in the U.S., Canada, Caribbean and Mexico.

4. You can earn 600 Qantas Frequent Flyer points for every qualifying stay at any Choice hotel in the United States, Canada, Caribbean, or Mexico.
5. You can earn 3 Qantas Frequent Flyer points for every Australian dollar charged to your room for qualifying stays in Australia or 600 Qantas Frequent Flyer points at any Choice hotel in New Zealand, Singapore, Papua New Guinea, Fiji, American Samoa and New Caledonia.
6. You can only earn airline rewards in one airline programme per qualifying stay.
7. Airline rewards can only be earned by one person per room per stay.
8. A "stay" is defined as any number of consecutive nights at one hotel regardless of check-ins or check-outs.
9. You must pay for and occupy the room in order to receive rewards.
10. If your individual hotel bill is billed directly to a company and you are responsible for authorization for settlement at check-out, your stay is eligible for airline rewards. However, group master-billing arrangements where charges for multiple rooms are placed on one hotel bill and billed to a company or common address or settled at check-out by one individual are not eligible.
11. Airline rewards are earned on the following standard rate plans (SRPs): Rack, Corporate (SCR), VIP Rates (SPC), Net Preferred (SNP), Government/ Military (SGM), 50+ Mature Traveler (SSC), Traveler's Discount (STD), AAA (S3A), Inn-to-Inn (SII), Small/Significant Organisation Savings

(SSO), Sixty Plus Rate (SSV), Sports Rate (LSPRT), CPSA (LR7), Negotiated Rates (N) and select LSRPs (LBEST, LHOME, LNINE, LGDS, LPCT, LCORP, LSTATE, LGO, L10, L15 and L20).

12. Allow 6-8 weeks for airline rewards to be credited to your frequent flyer account.
13. Once airline rewards have been credited to your designated frequent flyer account, they cannot be moved to another participating frequent flyer programme or be moved back to your Choice Privileges account.
14. Aeroplan®: Aeroplan is a registered trademark of Aeroplan Limited Partnership. Aeroplan terms and conditions subject to change without notice.
15. Alaska Airlines: All terms of Alaska Airlines Mileage Plan programme apply.
16. American Airlines: American Airlines reserves the right to change the AAdvantage® programme at any time without notice or to end the programme with six months notice. American Airlines is not responsible for products or services offered by other participating companies. For complete details about the AAdvantage program®, visit www.aa.com/advantage. AmericanAirlines® and AAdvantage® are trademarks of American Airlines, Inc.
17. Continental Airlines: All OnePass programme Terms and Conditions apply. Please visit continental.com/onepass for more details.
18. Delta Airlines: Please allow 6-8 weeks for miles to post to your account. All SkyMiles programme rules and conditions apply. To review the current SkyMiles Membership Guide and Programme Rules, please visit delta.com/skymiles. Delta, SkyMiles, and the Delta logo are registered service

marks of Delta Corporate Identity, Inc. Delta is not responsible for goods or services offered by any other company participating in this promotion.

19. Mexicana de Aviación: All Frecuenta programme terms and conditions apply.
20. Northwest Airlines®: Participation in Northwest airlines WorldPerks is subject to the terms and conditions of the WorldPerks programme.
21. Qantas: You must be a member of the Qantas Frequent Flyer programme to earn and redeem points in accordance with the Terms and Conditions of the Qantas Frequent Flyer programme. A joining fee applies.
22. Southwest Airlines®: Southwest Airlines Rapid Rewards Members must provide their account number to receive 0.5 credits per stay. All Southwest Airlines Rapid Rewards rules and regulations apply. Rapid Rewards credits will be deposited into the account within 4-6 weeks.
23. United: Miles accrued and rewards issued are subject to the terms and conditions of the United Mileage Plus programme.
24. US Airways®: All US Airways Dividend miles terms and conditions apply.

Hotel Benefits at U.S. and Canadian Properties

1. You may use Choice's express check-in service when you guarantee your reservation in advance with your credit card.
2. Local calls (except directory assistance and toll calls) and incoming faxes are free.
3. You will receive a complimentary *USA TODAY*, *The Wall Street Journal* or the *National Post* weekday newspaper. Or, a daily local newspaper if *USA TODAY*, *The Wall Street Journal* or the *National Post* is not available.

4. You may request a late check-out up to 2 p.m. local hotel time, as long as you do so at the hotel before the posted check-out time.
5. If you do not receive a Programme service at the hotel, you must advise the front desk staff of the problem right away and give them a chance to make the situation right. If the hotel staff is unable to satisfy you, Choice will determine the value of that service and seek the best way to provide you with a comparable value service or credit you a maximum of one night's room rental.
6. With *Choice Privileges*, you may enjoy the following Hotel Benefits at most of our hotels worldwide: discounted rates and extended check-out two hours past the standard time. Point or airline reward earning is not available at these locations.

Choice Privileges Rewards

1. Rewards are subject to room or specific reward availability and hotel participation.
2. Choice may periodically modify the Programme, with or without notice, by adding, changing or deleting Rewards, Points given, Reward thresholds, participating hotels or travel partners. If Choice modifies the Programme, you may not be able to obtain Rewards previously promoted.
3. You are responsible for any tax liability and disclosure obligations related to your Points, airline rewards and Rewards.

Choice Privileges Reward Nights

You may redeem a free night for as little as 6,000 points. Reward nights are available in the following tiers: 6,000, 8,000, 10,000, 12,000, 16,000, 20,000 and 25,000.

1. You must make your free room night reservations personally through the Programme Line or through your online profile no more than 30 days prior to your planned arrival for stays in the U.S and Canada or 60 days prior to your planned arrival at all other locations worldwide.
2. Your free room night does not include incidental charges and taxes.
3. The hotel will hold your room reservation until 7:00 am on the day after your scheduled arrival.
4. You may cancel your reservations through the Programme Line or through your online profile and by the date and time specified by your reservation sales representative or online.
5. If you are unable to use your room and fail to cancel your reservation, or if you do not claim the room by the specified time, Choice will not credit your account with the Points that you redeemed for that room.
6. You will not earn Points or airline rewards for free night stays.
7. You may not reserve free night stays through a travel agent, and free night stays are not commissionable to travel agents.
8. You may find the reward level for any participating hotel at choiceprivileges.com or by calling the Reservation Programme Line.
9. Choice may change the reward levels or level of any hotel at any time without notice.

Preferred Hotels & Resorts

1. You must make your free room night reservations personally through the Choice Service Center, Monday through Friday, 8 am - 10 pm EST no

more than 30 days in advance for locations in the U.S. and Canada and 60 days in advance at all other locations.

2. You may make your reward night reservation up until the date of arrival, but it must be done during the Choice Service Center's hours of operation, Monday through Friday, 8 am - 10 pm EST.
3. The cancellation policy of the selected Preferred Hotels & Resorts hotel applies to the *Choice Privileges* reward night and supercedes *Choice Privileges* programme rules.
4. Your free room night does not include incidental charges.
5. You will not earn any Points or airline rewards for free night stays.
6. Choice may change the amount of *Choice Privileges* points required for a free night of any hotel at any time without notice.
7. You will not earn any *Choice Privileges* points and/or airline rewards by staying at Preferred Hotels & Resorts properties.

Airline Rewards Redemption

1. You must be a member of a participating airline programme and abide by that program's rules and regulations to exchange *Choice Privileges* points for airline rewards.
2. You may redeem 5,000 Points for 1,000 miles with Air Canada Aeroplan®, Alaska Airlines Mileage Plan, American Airlines AAdvantage® programme, Continental Airlines OnePass®, Delta SkyMiles®, Frecuenta by Mexicana, Northwest Airlines® WorldPerks®, United Mileage Plus® or US Airways® Dividend Miles® or for 2.0 Southwest

Airlines Rapid Rewards® credits by calling the Choice Service Center at 888.770.6800 and providing your frequent flyer number.

3. Airline rewards cannot be exchanged for *Choice Privileges* points.
4. Allow 6-8 weeks for airline rewards to be posted to your airline account when redeeming *Choice Privileges* points for airline rewards.
5. Changes, reissuance or recredit of *Choice Privileges* points is not allowed once you have made a request to exchange *Choice Privileges* points for airline rewards.

Gift Certificates

1. To request redemption of your Points for a Gift Certificate, call the Choice Service Center or visit choiceprivileges.com.
2. Choice will mail your requested Gift Certificate rewards package by Postal Mail. You should allow two weeks from your request for delivery.
3. You may redeem your Gift Certificate for its face value, before its expiration date, and for merchandise or services only and not for cash.
4. You may not redeem an altered, changed or expired Gift Certificate.
5. Choice will not reissue Gift Certificates, even if lost or stolen.

Charitable Donations

1. To redeem points for a charitable donation, call the Choice Service Center or visit choiceprivileges.com.
2. Payments will be made to each charity on a monthly basis.

3. The donation will be reflected on your quarterly *Choice Privileges* statement which will constitute your receipt.
4. Please consult your tax advisor regarding whether your donation of points may be tax deductible.

Choice Service Center

You may phone the Choice Service Center, Monday - Friday, 8 am - 10 pm EST, or write the Choice Service Center at: 2697 U.S. Highway 50, Grand Junction, CO 81503. You may also send the Choice Service Center a fax at 970.257.1062. Please be sure to include your Member number on all correspondence.

Member Record Changes

1. You are responsible for advising Choice through the Choice Service Center of any name change. You must provide Choice with supporting written legal documentation, including your signature and Member number, plus the date of your request, for name change requests.
2. You are responsible for advising Choice through your Online Profile or the Choice Service Center of any changes in your contact information including address, phone number or email address.

Other Terms and Conditions

1. Choice may add, modify or delete Programme terms or conditions with or without notice, and may terminate the Programme at any time.
2. You may not transfer your points to anyone or by any means, including through a will or divorce decree.
3. You may not combine your Points with Points belonging to anyone else, including your spouse.

4. You may only maintain one Programme account. If you open more than one Programme account and have more than one Membership number, Choice will credit Points to only one account and terminate the other.
5. You may not sell or barter Points or redeem Points for cash.
6. Choice may modify the Points listed in your Programme account based on actual stay information.
7. If you have questions about a Programme statement, stay, or Points for a stay, you must contact the Choice Service Center within 60 days of the statement date. You must provide the Choice Service Center with your hotel receipt indicating your paid stay, plus your Member number, and other appropriate and unaltered documentation. Once received, please allow up to 15 days to process your request.
8. You should retain all stay documentation until you receive your Programme quarterly statement showing that Choice credited Points to your Programme account.
9. You will receive a quarterly statement either via mail or electronically only when you have earned or redeemed Points during the previous quarter.
10. You are responsible for understanding the Programme rules, tracking your Points and maintaining the security of your account.
11. Choice and its travel partners are not responsible for delayed, lost or misdirected mail, quarterly statements or other correspondence.
12. If you do not earn Points during 3 consecutive months, Choice may remove you from the Program's active mailing list.

13. If you have no activity for a period of 18 consecutive months, Choice may remove you from the Programme and therefore terminate your account. If Choice removes you from the Programme, you will forfeit your Points.
14. Choice may terminate the programme at any time without prior notice.
15. If Choice terminates the programme, you must redeem your Points for Rewards and complete your Reward stays within six months after the Programme End to avoid forfeiting your Points.
16. Choice and its partners at their discretion can terminate your membership and/or cancel some or all of your points, airline rewards or other rewards accrued or issued at any time and may take appropriate administrative and legal action if you abuse, violate or defraud the Programme, Membership Guide, Membership application, reservations or Hotel Benefits, Points or Reward redemption, or any federal, state or local law.
17. Choice may, in its sole discretion, revoke your Membership and Points if you do not pay outstanding Choice brand hotel accounts when due.
18. The Programme and/or Point rewarding or redeeming is void where prohibited by law.
19. The Programme will be governed by Maryland law, without regard to Maryland conflicts of laws principles.
20. You agree that Choice has the sole discretion to interpret all Programme rules and regulations and you hereby agree by your participation in the programme to abide by Choice's interpretations of these rules.

Privacy

1. Choice respects the privacy of its Members and is committed to protecting your personal information. When you become a Member, Choice and its affiliates collect information that you supply, such as your name, address, telephone number, e-mail address, room preference, and billing information. Choice and its affiliates use and share personal information about Members in order to administer Members' accounts and to offer and provide rewards, benefits, products, goods, and services to Members in connection with the Programme. "Affiliates" are companies that are owned or controlled by Choice, including Choice Hotels Canada, Inc. and Choice Hotels de Mexico.
2. Choice and its affiliates may share personal information with third parties engaged to assist them in providing services to you or to carry out one of the business purposes described above. These service providers are prohibited from using your personal information for any purpose other than to provide this assistance and are required to protect personal information disclosed by Choice.
3. If you elect to earn airline rewards or other benefits with Programme partners or redeem Points for Programme partner rewards, you authorize Choice and its affiliates to share your personal information with such Programme partners to the extent necessary to complete your request.
4. To the extent required or permitted by law, Choice and its affiliates may collect, use and disclose your personal information in connection with security related or law enforcement investigations or in the course of cooperating with authorities or complying with legal requirements.

5. By becoming a Choice Privileges Member, you authorize Choice and its affiliates to contact you via e-mail and postal mail with Programme administrative and transactional information.
6. Choice and its affiliates may occasionally contact you via e-mail and postal mail about Programme promotions, special offers, discounts, airline miles bonuses, or contests. If you would prefer not to receive these communications, you may instruct Choice to remove your name and address as specified.
7. Choice and its affiliates may occasionally share your personal information for marketing purposes to companies that are business associates, which may include airlines, hotels, retailers, telecommunications companies, credit card companies, banks and financial institutions, affinity membership programme operators, restaurants, tradeshow operators, magazines and other publishers, and charitable organisations. For Canadian residents, only basic contact information will be disclosed. You may instruct Choice not to share your personal information as specified
8. Subject to reasonable notice, you may withdraw your consent and opt-out of receiving promotions and offers as described in #6 above or having your personal information shared with business associates as described in #7 above by one of the following methods:
9. For Canadian Residents Only: If you have any questions or complaints about our privacy policies and practices, please e-mail us or write to us at Privacy Officer, Choice Hotels International Legal Dept, 10750 Columbia Pike, Silver Spring, Maryland USA 20901. You are entitled to gain

access to the information about you held by Choice and its affiliates, subject to the restrictions provided by law, and you may request rectification of inaccurate or incomplete information. If applicable, Choice will disclose this information to the person concerned or rectify it promptly. In order to gain access to your personal information, please contact our Privacy Officer as described in this #9

7

Issues of Hospitality Ethics

> Few of us realize how short the career of what we know as "science" has been. Three hundred and fifty years ago hardly any one believed in the Copernican planetary theory. Optical combinations were not discovered. The circulation of the blood, the weight of air, the conduction of heat, the laws of motion were unknown; the common pump was inexplicable; there were no clocks; no thermometers; no general gravitation; the world was five thousand years old; spirits moved the planets; alchemy, magic, astrology imposed on every one's belief.
>
> —*Some Problems of Philosophy*

One such book is by Hall (1992) entitled Ethics in Hospitality Management. In such cases, individual studies on determining important ethical issues become important tools to decide what to be included in a hospitality ethics course. Enghagen and Hott (1992) suggest that important and influential ethical issues must be identified so that students can discuss relevant issues in the industry. It is necessary that the content of the course is closely linked to real-world situations. That is the main reason why this study emphasizes seeking the industry's input in designing the content for a hospitality ethics course.

Among the few studies done in the USA, Enghagen and Hott (1992) concluded that hospitality students perceived pollution (air/water), solid waste disposal, conditions of employment, non-specific employment discrimination, race discrimination, employee theft and sex discrimination as the most compelling ethical issues in the industry. Subsequently, Weaver et al. (1997) conducted a similar research that also asked students to rank 24 ethical issues in accordance with their degree of importance in the industry. The results of the study have noticed similar findings. The students expressed condition of employment, solid waste disposal, pollution, sexual harassment and employee theft as the five most important issues.

Apart from soliciting views from the hospitality students, Vallen and Casado (2000) conducted a questionnaire survey with 45 hotel general managers. Respondents were asked to rank 12 ethical characteristics in terms of the importance they perceive such ethical characteristics have on the successful operation of their hotel. The findings reported that leadership is ranked the most important ethical characteristic, followed in descending order by accountability, commitment to excellence, integrity, honesty, fairness, law abiding, respect for others, promise keeping and trustworthiness, reputation and morale, loyalty and finally, concern for others.

It is evident that the few studies so far on discussing the importance of various ethical issues involved mainly the participation of hospitality students and general managers. It is apparent that there is a general lack of research that attempts to solicit views from staff members of different organisational levels in the industry. They are the ones who are involved in the day-to-day operation of the industry and are able to provide a wider spectrum of perspective and insights on the issue.

Hospitality Education

In descending order how the respondents ranked the degree of importance of the factors – "environmental protection" (4.41), "social conscience and employee integrity" (4.21), "social justice" (4.20), "consumer protection" (4.15), "business fraud" (3.90), "employee equity" (3.86), "privacy of employees" (3.72) and finally "personal advantage" (3.56).

The top three most important factors could be appropriately grouped together and renamed "accountability to society". Similarly, since the fourth and fifth most important factors are related to the moral ethics responsibility of an establishment to its consumers and guests, they could be considered together and renamed "accountability to external customers". The last three factors that were perceived to be relatively less important could be grouped under the heading "accountability to internal customers" as they were issues concerning individual employees. From the rankings determined by the factor mean analysis, it was concluded that industry practitioners consider ethics concerning accountability to society as the most important, followed closely by accountability to external customers and finally accountability to internal customers.

Methodology

This study used a self-administered and undisguised questionnaire, containing two sections, as the research instrument. The first section consisted of 39 ethical issues originating from the ethical issues rating scale developed by DuFrene et al. (1990). The original scale had short descriptions of 52 business issues of significance in business ethics. To ensure that the issues were relevant to the hospitality industry, a questionnaire with 55 issues (the 52 original issues plus three issues added by the researcher) was given to 20 academic staff of the School of Hotel and Tourism Management at the Hong Kong Polytechnic University for review and comments. They were asked to answer either "yes" or "no" for each issue; a "yes" answer indicated that the issue was applicable to the industry and should be included. If the percentage of affirmative answers was less than 50 percent, the issue would be deleted.

Using this dichotomous selection test, a total of 16 issues were excluded, and only 39 issues remained in the questionnaire. Respondents were asked to indicate the importance they perceived of each issue using a five-point scale, ranging from "1" for extremely unimportant to "5" for extremely important. As suggested by DeFrene et al. (1990) and Thomas et al. (1984), if an ethical issue is judged to be "important", it can be included as a study unit of a course. In this way, it was hoped that the study would be useful in shaping the ethics curriculum in hospitality. The second section of the questionnaire collected demographic information about the respondents, such as gender, age, years of work experience, organisational level as well as the department of the respondent.

Since the objective of the study was to collect views from industry practitioners, in January 2001, ten questionnaires were sent to each human resources manager or group director of 78 hotel companies in Hong Kong which represent all 91 member hotels of the Hong Kong Hotels Association. Each manager or director was requested to distribute the questionnaires to their staff for completion. Only 180 questionnaires were returned. Owing to the low response rate, reminder letters were sent to the hotels and follow-up calls were made.

An additional 128 questionnaires were received by the end of June 2001. Initial analysis of the raw data included a summary of means and standard deviations of the demographic information of the respondents and results of the survey of the 39 ethical issues. The mean scores were used to calculate the central tendency measure of the degree of importance of the statements and the standard deviations to explain the dispersal of scores around them. Factor analysis was adopted to define a set of common underlying dimensions among the 39 issues. Factors were formed to maximize their explanation of the entire variable (Hair et al., 1995).

Mean Scores and Standard Deviations for the 39 Ethical Issues

Each of the 39 issues received a mean score of more than 3 with an average mean score of 3.98. These results indicate that they are all perceived to be important in the hospitality industry from the industry's perspective. The four issues that received the highest mean scores were "theft of company property by employees" (4.48), "sexual harassment on the job" (4.45), "disposal of hazardous waste" (4.43) and "acceptance of bribes or gifts by employees" (4.40). At the same time, the four issues that received the lowest mean scores were "solicitation of tips from guests" (3.36), "hiring practices based on personal connections and favours" (3.63), "use of electronic tracking devices to monitor computer use by employees" (3.65) and "provide free/discount services to friends/relatives without the company's knowledge" (3.70).

Family Values

It is possible to draw some basic parallels between managing a hospitality firm and parenting in an archetypal nuclear family. It is clear that both are complex and long-term activities which depend upon myriad factors and in which success cannot always be assured. Effective hospitality management is a difficult activity which works best in stability, but which, in modern times, usually operates in dynamic markets and environments. Although there may be many units like the Halcyon Hotel in the hospitality industry, there are many more that muddle through in difficult, turbulent circumstances. Brian Cade might reflect that all was well today at the Halcyon, but as a good manager he would realise that tomorrow is another day, which would again demand his best efforts. Faced with a bad customer complaint, poor business results or the unexpected resignation of a key manager, his good humour would soon evaporate In real life, there is no endless supply of committed and trained staff as well as rich and easy to please customers.

Parents and hospitality managers might treat staff and guests equally, but responses will vary enormously. Some guests will be highly satisfied with the product and service, while others will complain. Similarly, some staff will take to the culture of the organisation and respond to development, while others will not perform effectively. Why do "children" who are treated similarly turn out differently? Are the "parents" or "children" to blame, or both? Some may find the family atmosphere unsuitable and stifling. Perhaps there are transferable core skills which operate in relationships in such diverse activities as coaching, mentoring, counselling and marriage. These might include such behavioural and altitudinal aspects such as respect, listening and empathy. Clear speaking and setting boundaries are also important in relationships. While general principles and parallels are useful, it is clear that each business or familial setting and circumstances is different and what works for one may not work for another. Is it possible to create conditions in which family-style co-operation and loyalty flourishes, or does this come about by chance?

It is clearly the responsibility of the hospitality manager to try and create these conditions, but the reward-effort bargain requires a formality of relationship and the adoption of roles must be in keeping with management style. It would be false and insincere if a naturally nervous or autocratic manager tried to adopt a paternalistic and caring role: employees would soon see this as a sham. Nevertheless, there may be room in the hospitality palette for more colourful and different organisational structures and arrangements. TGI Friday in the UK, for example, encourage an informal and theatrical atmosphere, and the Accor Group incorporates teamworking dialogue into its work practices.

Hospitality Ethics: Discussions

Although the 39 ethical issues examined in this study did not constitute by any means an exhaustive list of concerns in the hospitality industry, the study helps to identify the importance of each issue within the parameters given. This information is useful as a basis to develop a hospitality ethics curriculum. It is recommended that developers of hospitality curricula should consider the inclusion of these ethical issues in their programmes. For example, "theft of company property by employees" (4.48), "sexual harassment on the job" (4.45) and "disposal of hazardous waste" (4.43), "acceptance of bribes or gifts by employee" (4.40) and "provide fail-safe quality product/services" (4.37), the five most important issues identified, should receive priority in the curriculum, while other issues can be arranged and discussed sequentially in accordance with their importance to the industry. According to Taba (1962), the selection of content should meet the criteria of significance. It links to the matter of breadth and depth in the curriculum. From time to time, people find it difficult to maintain a suitable balance between the two, as there is always insufficient time. Thus, the identification of important issues in this study will help to form the basis of a hospitality ethics course. It represents a number of carefully selected topics that are significant to the subject being taught.

In the study of Yeung (2002), who surveyed the hospitality students in Hong Kong on the same 39 ethical issues similar results were found. The hospitality students rated "disposal of hazardous waste", "acceptance of bribes or gifts by employees", "sexual harassment on the job", "employees disclose corporate information or trade secrets" and "theft of company property by employees" as the top five most important issues. One point of caution is that the overall mean score of the 39 issues rated by the hospitality students is 3.82 when compared to 3.98 of the hospitality practitioners.

It can probably be interpreted as a stronger ethical awareness among the practitioners as they perceive most issues as relatively more important to the successful operation of the industry. As a matter of fact, the findings of this study also appear to corroborate the findings of some previous studies done in the USA (Enghagen and Holt, 1992; Weaver et al., 1997), in which "conditions of employment", "solid waste disposal", "sexual harassment", "employee theft" and "pollution of air and water" are found to be the important ethical issues. Apart from looking at individual issues, the curriculum design could be based on the results of the factor analysis.

In the analysis, the industry ranked "accountability to society" as the most important factor, followed by "accountability to external customers" and finally "accountability to internal customers"; hospitality educators could set the syllabus content with reference to these findings. There is also a strong correlation between the results of the factor analysis in this study and the categorization of Epstein (1989), who divided the analysis of ethics into four levels. The first level of analysis is macro-ethics pertaining to norms and values of the total political-economic system and encompasses issues such as environmental protection, social conscience and social justice, all of which were identified in this study. Epstein's second and third levels of analysis deal with the ethical conduct of an industry and of a firm towards its consumers and correspond to the fourth and fifth most important factors in the study, namely "consumer protection" and "business fraud"; both issues mainly relate to the ethical responsibility of an industry or a firm to its consumers. Finally, the last three factors in this study, "employee equity", "privacy of employees" and "personal advantage" can be equated to Epstein's final category, which addresses ethics of the individual.

Factor Analysis

This study adopted factor analysis to consolidate the 39 ethical issues into a set of underlying dimensions reflecting the perceptions of the industry of the various issues of ethics. For the purposes of quality control of the factors, the data were first tested using Barlett's test of sphericity, a statistical test for the overall significance of the correlations within a correlation matrix. The result of the Barlett's test was 4,064 (sufficiently high) with a significant level of 0.00. This indicates that factor analysis could be performed to further analyze the data. The final test conducted was the test of Kaiser-Meyer-Olkin (KMO), which is a measure of sampling adequacy. Hair et al. (1995) have claimed that data are valid if the value for the KMO test is found to be greater than 0.5. Since the value of KMO for the data in this study was found to be 0.866, it is concluded that factor analysis was valid in this study.

According to Hair et al. (1995), only those factors with eigenvalues or latent roots greater than 1 can be considered significant; all factors with values of less than 1 can be considered insignificant and should be discarded. This assumes that any individual factor should account for the variance of at least a single statement if it is to be retained for interpretation. The factor analysis used principal components with Varimax rotation and the eigenvalues for the eight factors in the data from this study, as indicated in the lower part, were all found to be greater than 1 and together they explained 50.48 percent of the cumulative variance. However, seven issues were deleted because their factor loadings were less than 0.5 and another three issues were discarded because there was only one issue in the factor.

1. Social Conscience and Employee Integrity

The second factor consists of seven issues, three of which were grouped under the heading "social conscience" as they deal with the value judgment as part of the policy and strategy of the company. However, erroneous decisions made on these issues do not necessarily constitute an offence against the law. These issues include "export of products that do not meet home country safety and/or quality standards" (4.02), "communication to public of sensitive information, e.g. bomb threats or product contamination" (4.25) and "remove a product from market due to potential health or safety risks" (4.23). Since the rest of the issues in this dimension are concerned with honesty and virtue of employees, they were categorized under the heading of "employee integrity". They include "theft of company property by employees" (4.48), "acceptance of bribes or gifts by employees" (4.40), "illegal copying of registered software" (3.91) and "employees disclosing company information or trade secrets" (4.21). A factor mean of 4.21, the second highest among the eight factors, suggests that the industry perceives this factor as a relatively important dimension of the hospitality industry.

2. Business Fraud

The first factor identified was named "business fraud" as five out of the seven issues in this dimension are related to criminal activities committed by employees. These issues include "use computers for illegal purposes" (3.94), "use investment capital from unknown or questionable sources" (3.94), "use insider business information for personal profit" (4.01), "disregard home country trade sanctions in the sale of goods, services and technology to foreign countries" (3.77) and "file overstated or false insurance claims" (3.98). These were all considered to be deliberate, illegal, law-breaking acts. An offence involving one of these issues would result in punishment by law.

3. Environmental Protection

Factor 3 comprises three issues that are closely related to the protection and enhancement of the environment and the community as a whole and was thus labeled as "environmental protection". The three issues in this dimension include "protection of natural resources" (4.04), "disposal of hazardous waste" (4.43) and "pollution of air and water" (4.32). This dimension recorded the highest factor mean of 4.41, reflecting the highest level of concern of the respondents about the impact of their industry on the ecological environment of society.

4. Personal Advantage

The fourth factor, "personal advantage", comprises three issues linked directly to people who take advantage of their positions in the company. The three issues in this dimension include "solicitation of tips from guests" (3.36), "provide free/discount services to friends/relatives without the company's knowledge" (3.69) and "hiring practices based on personal connections and favours" (3.63). The factor had the lowest mean of 3.56, indicating that it was perceived to be the least important factor. The result is possibly due to the fact that it does not have much impact on society and the company.

5. Consumer Protection

Factor 5 consists of two issues, "provide fail-safe quality products/services" (4.37) and "fair and complete media coverage of business issues" (3.92). This factor is concerned with the ultimate responsibility of the company to provide their customers with products and services that meet quality standards, and the fact that all consumers should have the right to be provided with complete information on products and companies so that they can make informed judgment prior to purchase or consumption of goods. A factor mean of 4.15, the fourth highest factor of the eight, evidently shows that this factor was fairly important.

6. Privacy of Employees

The two issues included in factor 6, "use of electronic devices to monitor employee activity on job" (3.79) and "use of electronic tracking devices to monitor computer use by employees" (3.65) refer to the invasion of employee privacy by a company and was therefore labeled as "privacy of employees". The factor has the second lowest mean of 3.72, indicating that comparatively it was not ranked very important among the eight factors.

7. Employee Equity

The three issues included in factor 7 relate to fairness in employment and compensation and benefits and could be appropriately named as "employee equity". These issues, "protection of specified groups by equal employment law" (3.92), "rights of employees to include funded child care, parental leave and elder care leave" (3.77) and "equal pay for comparable jobs" (3.90), state that it is a basic human right that everyone, regardless of color, race, religion or ethnic background, should be treated in the same manner and that all employees should be remunerated equitably in both compensation and benefits in accordance with their comparable worth. The factor mean was 3.86, the third lowest mean score among the eight factors, and it indicates that relatively speaking, it is not as important to the respondents.

Conclusions

Out of the 780 questionnaires distributed, 308 questionnaires were returned and this represents a response rate of 40 percent. The characteristics of the respondents; 41 percent were male and 59 percent female. Among these, 31 percent were aged 21 or less, while 45.2 percent were between the ages of 22 and 30; the age group of 31 and above represented 23.8 percent of the respondents. As for organisational level, 7.7 percent of the respondents belonged to senior management, i.e. executive committee members and department head (e.g. chief engineer, director of sales and marketing and front office manager). department head Bs (e.g. telephone manager, chief concierge, assistant housekeeping manager) represented 7.6 percent of the respondents, while supervisory and operative grades accounted for 84.7 percent of the respondents.

In terms of working departments, 20.7 percent of the respondents worked in the rooms division, while 61 and 13 percent worked in the food and beverage and administrative departments respectively (food and beverage departments included both service and production departments as well as banquet offices, while administrative departments included sales and marketing, human resources, accounts, engineering and managers' offices). Approximately 42.5 percent of the respondents had work experience of less than three years, while 34.7 percent had three to ten years of experience; only 22.8 percent of respondents had ten or more years of experience.

REFERENCES

Allam, Y.H., McGrath, M. (1996), "Assessing the readiness of Atlanta hotels to host international visitors during the '96 Summer Olympics", *FIU Hospitality Review*, Vol. 14 No.1, pp. 49-54.

Borchgrevink, C.P., Susskind, A.M. (1996), "The validity of the Hinkin and Schriesheim power scales and superior-subordinate power relationships within hospitality", *Hospitality Research Journal*, Vol. 20 No.1, pp. 39-56.

Diaz, P.E., Park, J. (1992), "The impact of isolation on hospitality employees' job satisfaction and job performance", Vol. 15 No.3, pp. 41-50.

Diaz, P.E., Umbreit, W.T. "Women leaders—a new, beginning", Vol. 18 No.3.

Dieke, P. (1990), "Fundamentals of tourism development: a third world perspective", Vol. 13 No.2, pp. 7-22.

Dienhart, J.R., Gregoire, M.B. (1993), "Job satisfaction, job involvement, job security, and customer focus of quick-service restaurant employers", Vol. 16 No.2, pp. 29-44.

Farber, B.M. (1994), "Hotel executive teams: balance of power among department heads?", Vol. 18 No.1, pp. 15-23.

Farmer, G. (1996), "A new vision: US travel and tourism industry", *FIU Hospitality Review*, Vol. 14 No.1, pp. 1-6.

Farrar, A.L., Murrmann, S.K., Vest, J.M. "Profiling managerial entrants to the hospitality industry", Vol. 18 No.1994, pp. 65-76.

Fenich, G.G. (1993), "Localized ground transportation in the 21 st century and its impact on the hospitality industry", Vol. 17 No.1, pp. 195-208.

Fenich, G.G. (1996), "The uses and abuses of multipliers: a current case", *Hospitality Research Journal*, Vol. 20 No.1, pp. 101-8.

Fletcher, B.C. (1988), "The epidemiology of occupational stress", in Cooper, C.L. , Payne, R. (Eds),*Causes, Coping and Consequences of Stress at Work*, John Wiley & Sons, Chichester,.

Francese, P. (1993), "Breaking the rules: delivering responsive service", Vol. 16 No.2, pp. 55-74.

Gilmore, S., Robson, R.A. (1990), "Student perception of laboratory experiences in quantity food production management", Vol. 14 No.1, pp. 101-16.

Go, F., Choi, T., Chan, C. (1996), "Four Seasons-Regent: building a global presence in the luxury market", *Cornell Hotel and Restaurant Administration Quarterly*, Vol. 37 No.4, pp. 58-65.

Godbey, G. (1993), "Time, work and leisure: trends that will shape the hospitality industry", Vol. 17 No.1, pp. 49-58.

Goll, G. (1989), "Management by values: consistency as a predictor of success", Vol. 14 No.1, pp. 55-68.

Grant, Y.N.J., Weaver, P.A. (1996), "The meeting selection process: a demographic profile of attendees clustered by criteria utilized in selecting meetings", *Hospitality Research Journal*, Vol. 20 No.1, pp. 57-72.

Murphy, J., Forrest, E., Wotring, C.E. (1996a), "Restaurant marketing on the world wide web", *Cornell Hotel and Restaurant Administration Quarterly*, Vol. 37 No.1, pp. 61-71.

Murphy, J., Forrest, E.J., Wotring, C.E., Brymer, R. (1996b), "Hotel management and marketing on the internet: an analysis of sites and features", *Cornell Hotel and Restaurant Administration Quarterly*, Vol. 37 No.3, pp. 70-82.

Murphy, M.M. (1990), "Vocational career testing contributes to student retention in hospitality programmes", Vol. 14 No.1, pp. 133-8.

Syrotnick, J.M., D2 Arcy, C. (1982), "Occupational stress, locus of control and health among men in a prairie province", *Canadian Journal of Behavioural Science*, Vol. 14 No.2, pp. 122-33.

Tarras, J.M. (1996a), "Using tax incentives reduces construction costs", *FIU Hospitality Review*, Vol. 14 No.1, pp. 55-8.

Williams, C.E. (1996), "The british pub—an industry in transition", *Cornell Hotel and Restaurant Administration Quarterly*, Vol. 37 No.6, pp. 62-73.

8

Hotel and Hospitality Industry and Facilities Management (FM)

> Undertake something that is difficult; it will do you good. Unless you try to do something beyond what you have already mastered, you will never grow.
>
> —*Ronald E. Osborn*

It is made all the more vexatious (and, it might be argued, even more interesting) by the evident growth of facilities management practice and international FM organizations dedicated to research and the dissemination of best practice. It is thus legitimate to inquire as to how facilities management can be practised in the absence of any definition as to what it is that is being practised. This is no mere sophistry, as will be demonstrated shortly. The principal objective of this paper is to explore issues in the definition of "FM" while drawing parallels with similar debates in other fields of vocational education, specifically hospitality management. The choice of hospitality management as a comparator is not arbitrary.

Like FM education, it is, in Europe, a relatively recent presence in institutions of higher education. Hospitality management is, like FM, a broadly vocational field with its origins in other, more established disciplines (many FM courses have their roots in professional engineering. Hospitality management has also faced problems of definition and acceptance within the wider academic community. Comparisons can thus potentially be instructive.

In the film of Umberto Eco's *The Name of the Rose*, competing religious factions meet in a remote monastery to debate whether Christ owned the clothes he wore. This situation finds resonance in academic life where, periodically, various disciplines and subject areas have experienced debates over the legitimate focus of their study.

In the UK, for example, Carr's (1961) book *What Is History?* had a profound influence upon discussions of no less than what should be constituted and taught as history. In the 1980s, Cambridge's English Faculty was riven by debates over the relevance of "structuralism" to the curriculum that led to the departure of a young academic, Colin McCabe. Nor are such controversies confined within disciplines. Various academics in the so-called "social studies of science" movement have challenged, or been perceived as challenging, the very basis of scientific theorising and technique (Collins and Pinch, 1993).

For the most part, these subjects are established "traditional" areas of the university curriculum. FM is not. One of a number of relatively new "vocational" subjects, there is debate over not only the definition of the subject, but also its scope. One suggested way of overcoming this lack of clarity is suggested by Jorna (1999, p. 44) who confidently asserts that: Although there is a common understanding about core competencies of FM, harmonizing educational programmes around them will be neither easy or, perhaps, necessary.

The precise balancing of competencies could be a distraction. Facilities management is still very new and still ill defined. This lack of definition is better seen as, not fluidity, but diversity. Perhaps a more productive approach would be to concentrate on understanding the essentials of facilities management. How do they translate into practical skills and individual qualities? The "core competencies" to which Jorna alludes are those developed and disseminated by the EuroFM organization Education Group. Derived *inter alia* from a review of existing FM course provision and professional pronouncements (from organizations such as the British Institute for Facilities Management) (Jorna, 1999, p. 43).

Careful consideration of these semi-official observations by Jorna highlights three problems of logic. The first has already been mentioned – how is it possible to talk meaningfully about facilities management if it remains impossible to define? Second, following Jorna's suggestion, how is it possible to concentrate on the "essentials" of FM if no agreement exists as to what is constituted by the study and practice of FM? Third, it seems that the second problem is to be overcome in terms of elaborating core competencies, which may or may not be the same as the "essentials of facilities management" to which Jorna (1999) alludes.

The problem here is that the first four core competencies developed by EuroFM are generic business and management competencies. Only in the management of premises and services is anything distinctive mooted. Even here, the competencies described could apply equally to managers in almost any service industry, for example retailing or hospitality. The difficulties are compounded when considering van Wagenberg's (1997) seminal paper on this topic. Reviewing various definitions of FM he contrasts US and Dutch approaches (the Dutch having played a major role in Europe in promoting the development of FM education). Two of the US definitions cited by van Wagenberg (1997, pp. 3-4) are of interest. FM is: The practice of co-ordinating the physical workplace with the people and work of the organization; it integrates the principles of business administration, architecture and the behavioural and engineering sciences (Cotts and Lee, 1992, p. 3, cited in van Wagenberg, 1997, p. 3). ... responsible for co-ordinating all efforts related to planning, design and managing buildings and their systems, equipment and furniture to enhance the organization's ability to compete successfully in a rapid changing world (Becker, 1987, p. 82, cited in van Wagenberg, 1997, p. 4).

The emphasis of both definitions is on co-ordinating but both definitions imply more than this – specifically that FM is a "throughput process" – it is invoked and implemented at the start of a building project and is an ongoing concern. Yet, as van Wagenberg (1997) demonstrates, such concerns have only relatively recently become a feature of FM practice – in short, historical evidence for FM as a throughput process is lacking. A further issue in van Wagenberg's (1997, p. 4) analysis arises from the aforementioned act of contrasting these US definitions with Dutch ones. The main difference emerges in the Dutch (and since, more broadly European) tendency to encompass all services within definitions of FM (e.g. reception, catering, security and mail handling). This produces very nearly the opposite of the problem thus far considered. It moves us from considering a term ("FM") in search of a meaning to defining that term in a manner so all-inclusive that it is nearly meaningless.

In the case of the definition recorded by van Wagenberg (1997) above, there is little that FM is not about. It is clear that existing debates over the definition of FM and its core competencies are flawed. Should we care? It might be argued that all new subject areas evolve organically and that facilities management is an emerging paradigm in any Kuhnian sense, one characterized by gradual growth interrupted by occasional, determining, revolutions (Kuhn, 1962). To have any hope of proposing an effective answer to this question, it is first necessary to examine what benefits might descend from greater clarity over the meaning of "facilities management". This exercise will be performed in three parts. First, the general academic environment in which FM and other vocational subjects operate will be considered. Second, parallels with a slightly more mature field of study – hospitality management – will be investigated. Finally, the possible lessons and future lines of enquiry to be drawn from such analysis will be considered.

One possible escape from deadlock is to reconsider the terms "facility" and "facilities" and perhaps distort the casual perception that the latter is simply the plural of the former, at least when "facilities" is linked to the term "management". If the review of ideas and issues in this paper show anything, it is that there is an ongoing tendency to professionalize and promote "FM" as a set of practices concerned with the management (defined in terms of integration and co-ordination) of buildings and building services. Also somewhat tentatively in the frame is an extension of this view, that FM embraces skills required at the inception of building design and subsequently throughout the whole construction process and operational cycle. In avoiding awkward arguments over definition it could be argued that FM practitioners have both submitted themselves to a "tyranny of relevance" and imposed an extremely restrictive if implied definition, of the singular term "facility".

Put simply, there is no *de facto* or logical imperative requiring us to equate a building with a facility. At the purely semantic level, the word "facility" is, for example, established in American English to refer to a group of buildings, a complex, as in "medical facility". rather than one building alone. More than this, however, it is demonstrably the case that certain elements or competencies embraced by FM can be delivered external to buildings, though rarely external to physical structures of some kind. In this sense therefore, a "facility" is a physical structure. Physical structures abound – bridges, railway lines, roads are all structures. A facility can be separated from other structures by reference to the manner of its usage (not necessarily purpose). That is, a facility is a structure that circumscribes or encloses physical space. Again, we are not much further forward – a cave encloses physical space but is little more use than as a cave. To complete our basic definition it is necessary to accept that a facility is generally an artificial, constructed structure, and to reflect on what, generically, can be regarded as the essence of such a structure.

One candidate fits this bill, namely the uses to which people put the structure, or more precisely human action. A facility is thus "a space enclosing physical structure, where the space and the structure are acted upon by humans for some purpose or purposes". This definition has the advantage of recognizing that a facility, like "hospitality" is not some universally given concept but a socially constructed one. The activities reviewed in this paper which form part of "FM" are not part of this definition.

To pursue an old cliché, FM as a concept is not part of the solution to how we define a facility, but rather is part of the problem. FM is an ideological process and set of competences which should, properly, be regarded as much as a subject of study as it is a set of professional practices. To use the jargon of sociology, it is necessary to adopt a reflexive approach to the practices of facilities management. These practices act upon a facility as much as the people who ultimately use that facility.

The above elaboration of some of the issues attendant on definitions of "FM" and the term "facility" are not intended to be didactic. Rather, the suggestion here is that there is merit in considering the divorce of the two, of unpacking the various practices that make up facilities management and treating them not only as practices *qua* practices, but as objects of inquiry in their own right. Such inquiry would be set against an essentially social scientific template of investigation into the nature of a "facility", recognizing the inherent flexibility with which humans and structures interact and develop. Much the same is happening (slowly) in the parallel field discussed here – hospitality and "hospitality management", with the latter being analysed relative to a template of what hospitality is, can or might be. None of this invalidates the set of practices that have become established as "hospitality management" but instead, understanding of the latter is enhanced and enriched by its location in a clear web of inquiry about the nature of hospitality. The same can be true for FM but only if the core concepts and processes at the heart of the field are systematically addressed.

The aim of this research undertaken in 1991, was to ascertain how the concept of total quality could assist in the more effective and efficient delivery of one aspect of health care in Northern Ireland, that of the provision of meals and domestic services to hospital patients. Traditionally the National Health Service did not focus on quality as a concept, but increasingly the provision of a quality service has become one of the corporate aims. This may be explained, in part, by the fact that Britain is part of the agreement as stipulated by the World Health Organization, which stated that by 1990 all member states should have effective mechanisms for ensuring the quality of patient care within their health care systems. The population of Northern Ireland has always received a high standard of health care and hospitals throughout the province have, in general, well-deserved reputations for responding to the health-care needs across the whole community. Since 1978, funding for health services in Northern Ireland had increased in real terms by almost 30 per cent, but annual hospital admissions had grown by 15 per cent to over 210,000 and almost 30,000 people received treatment annually as day patients. Such a reputation could not have been achieved without the continuing commitment of staff at all levels, but there was and still is, clear scope for improving the quality of promptness of the service that patients receive and the efficiency with which scarce resources are used. In addition to increasing the financial resources available, the government had, by 1991, already taken steps to improve quality standards, the most controversial of these being the introduction of a general management ethos into the National Health Service System.

A programme of action had been designed to secure the following objectives: to give patients, wherever they live, better health care and greater choice of the services available and to produce greater satisfaction and rewards for Health Service staff who successfully respond to local needs and preferences. In order to achieve these objectives, seven key measures were proposed and these included: more delegation of responsibility to local levels, self-governing hospitals, new funding arrangements, additional consultants, budgets controlled by general practitioners, better audit arrangements and reformed management bodies. It was also considered that the effectiveness of the service would be improved if, regional, district and family practitioner management bodies were reduced in size and reformed on business lines. In order to determine the quality of the meals and domestic services and the attitudes of the professionals in the industry providing these services a case study was undertaken on a major teaching hospital on the outskirts of Belfast. The methodology was in the format of formal interviews with senior personnel from the hospital to discover the background and working nature of the unit. Insight was also gained as to the past and present situation with regard to the quality of service provided. In order to test the validity of adopting TQM, it was necessary to evaluate the existing systems, to find out where strengths and weaknesses lie and if and how TQM could improve the quality of service and the quality of employees' working life. The method used to obtain this information was by the use of an attitudinal survey, which was carried out at management, supervisory and auxiliary levels within the following departments: Domestic Services, Catering, Laundry, Portering, and Maintenance.

The results of the research indicated that there were several areas which could be improved by the use of TQM techniques. It was estimated that if implemented the following benefits could be expected:

- There would be considerable cost reductions.
- Suggestions made by all levels of staff to improve communications and relations between management and staff would be realized and fulfilled.
- The general morale would be greatly improved as a result of the increased responsibility, motivation and involvement in the quality process. Perhaps these effects would help to reduce the levels of sickness and high

labour turnover which are typical of almost all hospital environments.

Human Resource Issues

Globalisation is, increasingly, preoccupying industry practitioners, academics and students in interrelated fields of hospitality, travel and tourism (Gannon and Johnson, 1995). As a result the number of texts focusing on human resources in the international context of hospitality, travel and tourism is steadily growing. While each of these texts has its merits, few of them concentrate on cross-sectoral analyses (Costa, 1995; Ingram, 1995). Further, none of the texts published to date combines mainstream human resource theory with the international context of hospitality, travel and tourism. To meet this market need, the authors of this piece are developing an edited text on international hospitality, travel and tourism organisations (*Human Resource Developments and Issues in International Hospitality, Travel and Tourism*, Cassell) for publication in 2002. This text will:

- analyse the contemporary theory on the nature of the management and development of human resources in these sectors;
- draw from a worldwide survey, undertaken for the text, on current human resource issues and priorities in international hospitality, travel and tourism organisations;
- include contributors' chapters which explore particular issues in relevant case organisations; and
- critically discuss emergent themes and exigent issues in contemporary and prospective human resource management in the specific context of international hospitality, travel and tourism.

The survey stage of the development of the text is now reaching completion. Some 472 international organisations (defined as operating in two or more countries) in every continent have been surveyed by the authors. The survey invited the most senior human resource specialist in each organisation to prioritise current and future (defined as the period 2001-2006) human resource issues. Inclusion of prospective issues is considered important as their identification offers some insight into the extent of forward planning for human resource issues. The potential issues – 35 in total – were specified in the questionnaire under the generic headings of Performance management, Labour markets, Managing change and Organisational Culture/Cross-cultural dimensions. In each category, respondents were asked to identify any other current/future human resource issues. Lastly, respondents were asked to indicate which issues are included in their organisation's strategic planning. A total of 67 questionnaires have been returned, representing over 300, 000 employees in countries around the world. These responses can be considered as indicative of international hospitality, travel and tourism organisations in general. Initial analysis of the questionnaire results reveals that for the surveyed organisations the issues highlighted.

Evidently, a wide range of human resource dimensions, spanning employee resourcing, development and relations, are significant at present to international hospitality, travel and tourism organisations. That these dimensions are significant is also indicated by their inclusion in the future issues identified by the respondents, albeit in a slightly different order of priority. The issues highlighted as prospectively important also include further human resource dimensions. Thus, in short, human resource issues are of central importance to international hospitality, travel and tourism organisations in terms of the range of issues, the dynamic nature of the issues and, at least potentially, their organisational impact.

Hotels increasingly emphasize specialized training. Postsecondary training in hotel or restaurant management is preferred for most hotel management positions, although a college liberal arts degree may be sufficient when coupled with related hotel experience. Internships or part-time or summer work are an asset to students seeking a career in hotel management. The experience gained and the contacts made with employers can greatly benefit students after graduation. Most bachelor's degree programs include work-study opportunities. Community colleges, junior colleges, and some universities offer associate's, bachelor's, and graduate degree programs in hotel or restaurant management. Combined with technical institutes, vocational and trade schools, and other academic institutions, over 800 educational facilities have programs leading to formal recognition in hotel or restaurant management. Hotel management programs include instruction in hotel administration, accounting, economics, marketing, housekeeping, food service management and catering, and hotel maintenance engineering. Computer training also is an integral part of hotel management training, due to the widespread use of computers in reservations, billing, and housekeeping management.

Additionally, over 450 high schools in 45 States offer the Lodging Management Program created by the Educational Institute of the American Hotel and Lodging Association. This is a two-year program offered to high school juniors and seniors, which teaches management principles and leads to a professional certification called the "Certified Rooms Division Specialist". Many colleges and universities grant participants credit towards a post-secondary degree in hotel management. Lodging managers must be able to get along with many different people, even in stressful situations. They must be able to solve problems and concentrate on details. Initiative, self-discipline, effective communication skills, and the ability to organize and direct the work of others also are essential for managers at all levels.

In the past, many managers were promoted from the ranks of front desk clerks, housekeepers, waiters, chefs, and hotel sales workers. Although some employees still advance to hotel management positions without education beyond high school, postsecondary education is preferred. Restaurant management training or experience also is a good background for entering hotel management, because the success of a hotel's food service and beverage operations often is important to the profitability of the entire establishment. Graduates of hotel or restaurant management programs usually start as trainee assistant managers. Some large hotels sponsor specialized on-the-job management training programs that allow trainees to rotate among various departments and gain a thorough knowledge of the hotel's operation. Other hotels may help finance formal training in hotel management for outstanding employees. Newly built hotels, particularly those without established on-the-job training programs, often prefer to hire applicants who have hotel management experience. Large hotel and motel chains may offer better opportunities for advancement than small, independently owned establishments, but relocation every several years often is necessary for advancement.

The large chains have more extensive career ladder programs and offer managers the opportunity to transfer to another hotel or motel in the chain or to the central office. Career advancement can be accelerated by the completion of certification programs offered by various associations. These programs usually require a combination of course work, examinations, and experience. For example, outstanding lodging managers may advance to higher level manager positions.

Job Outlook

Employment of lodging managers is expected to grow more slowly than the average for all occupations through 2012. Additional job openings are expected to occur as experienced managers transfer to other occupations or leave the labor force, in part because of the long hours and stressful working conditions. Job opportunities are expected to be best for persons with college degrees in hotel or restaurant management. Increasing business travel and domestic and foreign tourism will drive employment growth of lodging managers.

Managerial jobs are not expected to grow as rapidly as the hotel industry overall, however. As the industry consolidates, many chains and franchises will acquire independently owned establishments and increase the numbers of economy-class rooms to accommodate bargain-conscious guests. Economy hotels offer clean, comfortable rooms and front desk services without costly extras such as restaurants and room service. Because there are not as many departments in these hotels, fewer managers will be needed. Similarly, the increasing number of extended-stay hotels will temper demand for managers because, in these establishments, management is not required to be available 24 hours a day.

In addition, front desk clerks increasingly are assuming some responsibilities previously reserved for managers, further limiting the employment growth of managers and their assistants. Additional demand for managers is expected in suite hotels, because some guests—especially business customers—are willing to pay higher prices for rooms with kitchens and suites that provide the space needed to conduct meetings. In addition, large full-service hotels—offering restaurants, fitness centers, large meeting rooms, and play areas for children, among other amenities—will continue to provide many trainee and managerial opportunities.

Organizations in International Hospitality Business

Lockwood and Guerrier report on the benefits and problems arising from the adoption of flexible working practices. Sampling hotel operators, they investigated the current and future potential of functional, numerical and pay-related forms of flexibility and found comparatively little evidence of flexible working. Several years later, Luckock profiles the development of a flexible working programme for area catering supervisors in contract catering. She concludes that the role *can* be re-shaped in a more flexible way either by re-writing the job description, or by introducing flexible arrangements which do not change the structure of the job, but enable tasks to be conducted more easily. Both articles comment on the potential benefits of greater flexibility for employees and employers (especially for optimal work scheduling) yet in terms of implementing imaginative schemes for flexible working little progress appears to have been made.

The pace of innovation in working methods and practice is, to some extent, dependent on employee relations. Kelliher reviews management-employee relations with reference to developments in public and private sector catering. Riley approaches this issue by considering the impact of collective bargaining on labour utilization. He analyses collective agreements from six countries and considers the extent to which unionization affects the operational characteristics of hotels. Riley's analysis reveals two key points. First, that managers appear to lack control in unionized conditions and have fewer options than in a free market system. Second, that the more detailed union agreements used in the USA seem to offer more to management because there is less room for misinterpretation. He concludes that the first real challenge for collective bargaining is to reduce the level of dependence on traditional job classifications.

Reviewing terms and conditions for managers, Linney and Teare report on the role of flexible incentive packages in rewarding achievement. "Flexibility" in this instance refers to the relative attractiveness of incentive packages in different European countries. For instance, a non-contributory pension scheme in Germany is less attractive to younger managers who can opt for an alternative, such as an incentive based on a thirteenth-month salary bonus, a practice which is widely used in Germany. Kelliher and Blackman consider the potential implications of the European Social Charter for human resource strategy in the UK hospitality industry. They review four key areas: labour usage, the role of the law, management-union relations and technology. Commenting on the challenges for the hospitality industry they foresee that, in some areas, changes (such as increased worker participation) are likely to occur and that organizations will need to keep their manpower policy development plans under review to reflect this.

Lundberg and Woods note that the relationships between organizational culture and managerial work are especially important and that the sense of vitality and enthusiasm generated by the workforce critically depends on the maintenance of a supportive culture. They provide a framework for interpreting organizational culture and using examples drawn from a US restaurant chain, they identify the different managerial roles required to sustain a supportive organizational environment. Related points are made by Davis and by Dann as they discuss the role of managers in dealing with employees, business opportunities, technology and other factors which influence the relative stability of an organization's ethos and culture. Meudell and Gadd discuss the link between "strong" culture and organizational performance by reviewing the concepts of *culture*, generally viewed as a long-term, incremental process, and organizational *climate* as they apply to short-life hospitality organizations (see also Mullins *et al.* and Sinclair and Arthur). Organizational communications play a key role in the degree of supportiveness that employees experience. Larsen and Folgero examine the communication structure of a cruise company using a research instrument known as the communication climate inventory to gather data and interpret the implications for organizational climate, culture and traditions. An important aspect of effective two-way communication is the extent to which the organization "listens" to its employees.

Brownell notes that the listening environment is a key cultural influence, irrespective of the size and complexity of an organization. She examines the ways in which this aspect of the overall environment influences both the accomplishment of organizational tasks and the development of interpersonal relationships on the job. She observes that managers can deliberately control many aspects of the listening environment and that effective hospitality leaders deliberately create strong listening environments so as to increase employee participation, excellent guest service and organizational commitment

Riley discusses the main approaches to analysing the causes and effects of labour turnover and argues the case for a change of direction in the way writers, practitioners and researchers perceive the phenomenon of high labour turnover. Lucas considers the wider issue of industry employment patterns during the 1970s and 1980s. She foresees continued job growth throughout the 1990s, set against a changing labour force picture. It seems likely that rising job numbers will reflect more jobs for fewer hours rather than a real increase in full-time employment. In this scenario, a characteristic of labour utilization is likely to be "flexibility" as employers increase the ratio of part-time jobs so as to manage peaks and troughs in business demand more easily.

Investigating the motivational preferences of Caribbean hotel workers and the impact of individual differences on these preferences, Charles and Marshall conducted a survey in seven hotels in the Bahamas. Hotel workers were motivated most by higher wages but differences in age, organizational level and number of years in the same job position also influenced workers' motivational preferences. The article concludes by highlighting the need for managers to deploy both creative, monetary-based incentives and different motivational strategies for different groups of workers. Investigating a related issue, Lee-Ross reports a close link between management style and employee motivation. His study generally supports the hypothesis that "hands-on" managers score jobs similarly to their workers and that "co-ordinative" managers do not. Dodrill and Riley explore the motivational dimension of employee attitudes to work by studying the relative values that hotel workers place on job scope and autonomy. The literature suggests that these attributes are highly valued by workers but the study findings suggest that the relationship is less predictable than this.

Employee Selection and Personality Assessment

Waryszak and Bauer report that employee selection methods and techniques used in Australian hotels mainly rely on an application form and work references for screening purposes and one-to-one or small panel interviews for employee selection. Yet as Worsfold points out, this approach is known to be unreliable, partly because it fails to assess the fit between a candidate's personality characteristics and the job itself. Dickinson and Ineson offer a solution to this problem in the form of two more sophisticated selection techniques – biodata (biographical information) profiling and personality assessment. Both techniques have been found to have high predictive validities when used in other industries. In support of the use of biodata in hotel front-of-house employee selection, Ineson and Brown present findings of a pilot study which sought to improve the success rate of employee selection. The study, which reports promising results, involved the development and testing of a method for scoring applicants for operational front-of-house positions using biodata based on their interpersonal skills and their job flexibility.

9

Guidelines and Concerns in Quality Management

> Hospitality is a wonderful thing. Concern for the pleasure and comfort of a guest is an extremely admirable trait. However, I think the Eskimos carry it a little too far. As for example, when a man traveling alone stops for a period at the house of a friend, the host offers to share his wife with his guest . The offer usually is accepted. A refusal might be considered insulting. As women are somewhat scarce in the Arctic, wife-sharing is not unusual. At times, three or four Eskimos share a wife. They all live together. The men do the housework.
>
> —*E. V. Durling*

In recent years there has been an explosion of interest in quality management. Debates surrounding the most appropriate means of ensuring and enhancing the quality of products or services has recently been examined in the context of small hospitality firms by Church and Lincoln (1998). They begin by arguing that if small firms addressed the issue of quality management, they might expect to gain advantages over their competitors that should result in a more secure financial future. A central tenet of Church and Lincoln's work is the rejection of retrospective methods of quality control. They argue that such approaches, with their emphasis on comparing outputs with a given standard, are both expensive and highly intrusive in the context of services. As a result, they promote preventative systems of quality control.

Their proposition is that if the various stages of the process of production and/or service delivery are controlled, little, if any, testing of the final product or service is required. Against this background, they examine the potential of two methods: Hazard Analysis Critical Control Points (HACCP) and Failure Modes and Effects Analysis (FMEA). Both are seen as potentially valuable, but two limitations are recognised by the authors.

First, there has so far been little systematic evaluation of these systems in small hospitality firms. Consequently, their strengths and weaknesses in such environments remain to be tested.

The second is that the approaches are partial; they do not necessarily produce the holistic approach to quality management that many commentators now advocate. In order to overcome the second of these limitations, Church and Lincoln (1998) review a range of alternatives: Investors in People (IiP), benchmarking, BS EN ISO 9000, total quality management (TQM) and quality costing. They see potential merit in both IiP and quality costing.

In the current hospitality industry, guests are flocking to properties, management companies are becoming more stable, and owners are gathering renewed confidence in the industry. Properties enjoying profitability are those with the right mix of product, quality, price and servicE.-If the hospitality industry is to continue to meet the challenges of 1990s and beyond, quality management (QM) must become the way of life. Most customers are unwilling to pay for amenities they do not want and will avoid those properties where high rates are not clearly related to value. To improve services, hospitality organizations must focus on individual attributes and overall customer satisfaction. The purpose of this paper is to examine the issue of implementing QM programmes in the hospitality industry. The first of its three sections reviews the literature on QM in the hospitality sector and provides a synopsis of hospitality groups'/hotels' responses to this issue. The second section presents a strategic programming model to implementing QM in the hospitality industry. The five stages in the model include: awareness and commitment; planning; programming; implementation and evaluation. In the final section, issues relating to QM in the hospitality sector which need to be addressed in the future are suggested.

TQM (Total Quality Management)

This study will provide an overview of initiatives and trends, such as Quality Management and 'Investors in People', and how their development will affect human resource management in the future. If you study the lists of new publications connected with Quality Management and management principles in general, you will identify the preoccupation with such developments. Alongside various pieces of Government legislation and initiatives have emerged the so-called management gurus. Such individuals as Tom Peters, Professor Hardy and Sir Harvey Jones have become acclaimed as the prophets of business success. Studies and articles on Quality Management are commonplace, as are numerous one-day seminars and conferences. There is no doubting that issues related to quality management will be with us for some time. The trend towards developing quality management approaches and systems has also been helped by the following:

(i) the effects of European Union harmonisation and legislation

(ii) the effects of the recession in the late 1980s and early 1990s, which forced many organisations to focus its energies on retaining customer loyalty

(iii) the growth in other industrial sectors of quality management systems, such as BS5750 (UK version) and IS9000 (international version)

(iv) UK legislation, such as the Food Safety Act 1990 and various alterations to HASAWA legislation

(v) the influence of numerous management writers
(vi) initiatives such as 'Investors in People'

During the early part of the 1990s there was a growing recognition of the value and benefits of such approaches, reflected by the move towards customer-focused businesses. (You will have seen this trend by the content of company material within this text.) That is not to say that the concept of Quality Management is one which originated in the last decade. The Second World War provided an impetus to aspects of quality assurance as the Forces depended on equipment that worked 'first time every time'. Teachers and writers, such as Edward Deming, were influential in developing approaches to overall concepts of quality, a term later developed as Total Quality Management. Whilst the term Quality Management is not a new one, it has only been in the early part of the 1990s that the hospitality industry has moved towards the large scale implementation of its principles.

Quality management centres on the following aspects:

(i) systems and methods for assuring the quality of services, facilities and goods
(ii) development of the concept of continuous quality improvement
(iii) increasing focus of quality improvement via the involvement and empowerment of all employees
(iv) recognition that a team approach to maintaining and improving quality is the best strategy for customer-focused businesses
(v) quality improvement has as much to do with organisational culture change as it has with systems and processes

Of course quality is a term with many definitions; is it what the individual employee, department, unit or company perceive, or is the customer, the professional association or the restaurant the food critic? Certainly the rise in customer expectation over the past few years has altered their perception of quality. However, individual customers will have varying definitions of quality and may relate these to such factors as facilities, value for money, cost, or efficiency level of staff responsiveness and care. The recent debate amongst hotel operators over grading systems, which attempt to indicate a level of quality or facilities, shows just how difficult the definition of quality really is. With the development of external quality assessment and accreditation systems, the creation of benchmarks or minimum quality standards has become perhaps easier.

Customer Relationship and Service Quality

The main function which a hospitality organization's members must perform is the delivery of quality services to its customers. Eight articles from the *Hospitality Research Journal* discuss how employees can best deliver quality service to the organization's customers. Barsky (1996) suggests that customers may be excellent sources of information for management on how the organization can provide quality service. Through surveys and focus groups, customers can help management determine which service areas are most in need of improvement. Management may also choose to create an internal service-quality audit which can identify errors and determine their frequency, assign costs of fixing (or not fixing) the error, and identify the steps to prevent them.

Luchars and Hinkin (1996) described an example of such an audit conducted at a full-service hotel to determine the cost of errors in transactions at the front desk. The most common error was failure to post late charges to the guest's folio, which cost the hotel an estimated $250,000 per year. This internally and externally derived information can assist management in its endeavours to satisfy customers. Gunderson *et al.* (1996) defined customer satisfaction as, "a guest's post-consumption judgment of a product or service that can, in turn, be measured by assessing guest's evaluation of a performance on specific attributes". The research revealed that business travellers were most concerned with the tangible aspects of housekeeping (e.g. room amenities) and the intangible aspects of the front desk (e.g. receptionists' willingness to provide service). Being able to provide services which customers prefer is obviously a starting point for providing customer satisfaction. A relatively easy way to determine what services customers prefer is simply to ask them. Travellers who Greathouse stopped at visitor information centres rated cleanliness of room, value for price, friendliness of staff, and security of property as some of the most important attributes of a hotel.

In today's changing global environment, many businesses are facing intensifying competition and rapid deregulation, and in order to achieve competitive advantage and efficiency, businesses have to seek profitable ways to differentiate themselves. One strategy that has been related to success is the delivery of high service quality, especially during times of intensive competition both domestically and internationally (Rao and Kelkar, 1997). This concept has been the subject of many conceptual and empirical studies, and it is generally accepted that quality has positive implications for an organisation's performance and competitive position.

However, despite the vast amount of research done in the area of service quality, quality related issues have received little research attention within the hospitality context (Harrington and Akehurst, 1996). Further, authors of studies conducted on quality in the service industries have also expressed concern regarding the quality dimensions in hotels and, in particular, with methods used to measure customer perceptions of hotel service quality (Johnston *et al.*, 1990).

As service quality is becoming a major part of business practice, it is important to be able to measure and research its effectiveness. The purpose of this paper is to examine the different dimensions of service quality and determine which dimensions best predict overall service quality in the hospitality industry by applying a modified version of SERVQUAL (Parasuraman *et al.*, 1988). This kind of information has practical implications for managers of hotels as they can direct their resources to improving weak service dimensions and to refining their marketing efforts so that customer expectations are met by the service delivered.

Early Research on Quality

From the review of literature on quality, it has been found that early research efforts concentrated on defining and measuring the quality of tangible goods and products, while the seemingly more difficult services sector was ignored. Gronroos (1990) has noted that product quality was traditionally linked to the technical specifications of goods, with most definitions of quality arising from the manufacturing sector where quality control has received extensive attention and research. Conversely, Crosby (1979) defined quality of goods as "conformance to requirements"; Juran (1980) defined it as "fitness for use"; while Garvin (1983) measured quality by counting the incidence of "internal" failures (those observed before a product left the factory) and "external" failures (those incurred in the field after a unit had been installed). These product-based definitions of quality may be appropriate to the goods-producing sector, however, knowledge about the quality of goods is insufficient to understand service quality (Parasuraman *et al.*, 1985).

Services are generally described in terms of four unique attributes, namely:

- Intangibility;
- Heterogeneity;
- Inseparability; and
- Perishability

(Bateson, 1977; Lovelock, 1981; Gronroos, 1990; Zeithaml and Bitner, 1996). In the hospitality industry, other attributes, such as imprecise standards and fluctuating demand have been identified and further complicate the task of defining, delivering and measuring service quality. For example, while firms in the hospitality industry have established policies, rules and procedures to govern the standardisation of their product, many aspects of service quality do not lend themselves to standards. Quality aspects such as "friendliness", "helpfulness" and "politeness" are likely to be interpreted differently by various guests and are assessed subjectively. Moreover, demand for service in the hospitality industry is generally clustered around peak periods of the day or year, such as check-out time or holiday season (Sasser *et al.*, 1978) and these peaks create an environment which make it difficult to provide consistent service quality.

One of the most widely used instruments to measure service quality is the SERVQUAL scale developed by Parasuraman *et al.* in 1985, and then refined in 1988 and 1991. The model on which SERVQUAL is based proposes that customers evaluate the quality of a service on five distinct dimensions:

- Reliability;
- Responsiveness;
- Assurance;
- Empathy; and
- Tangibles

and that service quality is the difference between a customer's expectations and perceptions of the quality of a service. In order to operationalise this model, the authors developed 22 items that were designed to capture, in two separate columns, customers' perceptions and expectations of a service on those dimensions, making a total of 44 questions in all. Despite SERVQUAL's wide usage by academics and practicing managers in various industries, across different countries, a number of studies have questioned the conceptual and operational base of the model (Babakus and Boller, 1992; Carman, 1990; Teas, 1994). More specifically, these studies have failed to confirm the five dimension structure across different industries. For example, a study conducted in the hospitality industry reported five dimensions of service quality, and these differed from those in SERVQUAL (Saleh and Ryan, 1991). These findings suggest that further customisation of the scale for the hospitality industry is necessary. To address concern about the soundness of using a perceptions minus expectations score, researchers have combined the expectations and perceptions scores into a single measure. They subsequently found the reliability and validity of this single measure superior to the score based on the difference method (Babakus and Boller, 1992; Brown *et al.*, 1993). In 1991, Parasuraman *et al.* published their own one-column scale format which cuts the questionnaire size in half and reduces the time required for completion (Bouman and Van der Wiele, 1992), thus minimising the likelihood of response error.

The specific aims of the study are to:

- test the reliability and validity of a customised SERVQUAL scale;
- establish the number of dimensions of service quality in the hospitality industry; and
- determine which dimension is the best predictor of overall service quality.

In order to distinguish between the revised SERVQUAL (Parasuraman *et al.*, 1991) and the version customised for this study, the latter will now be referred to as HOLSERV.

Education

Alongside the issue of graduateness discussed above, the question of skills development has also become a priority area for those involved in vocational education, including the higher education sector. "Productivity and social cohesion are key twin challenges facing the UK in ensuring our nation's economic success in the twenty-first century. At the heart of both these challenges lies skills – for the competitiveness of our businesses and the employability of our people" (Humphries, 1998). The Skills Task Force has identified that both generic and vocational skills are necessary. Generic skills are defined as transferable skills including the key skills of communication, application of numbers, problem solving, team working, IT and improving own learning and performance.

They have also been defined as including reasoning skills and personal values and attitudes such as motivation, discipline, judgement leadership and initiative. Vocational skills are defined as the specific technical skills necessary to work within an occupation or occupational group, often those described within occupational standards. The skills debate is therefore very much a part of the graduateness debate. The role of the workplace in developing these skills is set to assume even greater importance. "There is set to be a renewed focus on how to improve the extent and quality of learning in the workplace" (Humphries, 1998, p. 9). The focus includes work-based learning during higher education, but also continuing professional development of the workforce as part of lifelong learning.

The high profile of the workplace as a focus for learning will build upon the extensive development of work based learning which took place as a result of the DfEE funded projects in the mid-1990s (Brennan and Little, 1996). Hospitality played a full part in such projects and in any event has a long history of developing enterprise skills through collaboration with industry.

These have often been via student learning activities based around industry problem solving and consultancy projects. Supervised work experience is also an integral part of many, but not all hospitality courses.

The Industry Tutors' Group works to ensure that this

aspect of students' learning experience is a positive and constructive one. Employers value supervised work experience as an excellent introduction to the world of work and as a means of instilling a sense of realism as to what the industry is about and the career opportunities which it offers. The period of work experience also provides an opportunity to develop key skills such as teamwork and communication and personal attributes such as persuasiveness and self-discipline. With the reduction in the unit of resource, there is likely to be continuing pressure to demonstrate that the placement period represents a cost-effective use of funds.

At the same time, the HCIMA as part of one of the DfEE sponsored Higher Education and Employment, Work Experience projects is investigating the extent of student part-time work in the hospitality industry (HCIMA, 1998). Pilot results from this project showed that around 90 per cent of first year hospitality students had undertaken part-time and/or vacation work in the industry. The HCIMA research also demonstrated that part-time student employees are a very important and convenient human resource for many hospitality businesses.

Students are available to work during seasons and times which enable many businesses to match the supply of labour to their peaks of business. It is not simply hospitality students, but students from many different undergraduate and graduate courses who are being employed. It is the generic skills of students and some previous experience of working in the industry which are sought, rather than an academic background in hospitality. The increased recognition as to the extent of student part-time work and the learning opportunity represented by it has important implications. Thames Valley University have already developed an accelerated Hospitality Management Higher Diploma Course which utilises students' part-time work experience as an alternative to a period of full-time supervised work experience.

The part-time employment of non-hospitality students in

front of house, customer oriented positions also gives cause for reflection as to whether the industry is really as reliant on the vocational skills component of hospitality degrees as some employers maintain. Certainly some employers are willing to accept practical expertise which has been gained by work experience rather than as part of a formal study programme. If change is in the air regarding the role of work based learning, it is as nothing compared to that which will surely be brought about by the increased use of technology in the learning process. In the short term it is the Internet which will be the preferred medium for the delivery of learning programmes. This enables students to engage in the learning process within virtual classrooms. These can provide learning which, though different from the face to face experience, is nevertheless very powerful.

As a geographically fragmented worldwide industry, hospitality is one of the vocational sectors most suited to this form of learning. Since the Internet knows no frontiers, there is an opportunity to reach large numbers of students without the requirement to invest in expensive satellite buildings. However, alternative expensive investment is required. Many of the UK universities have set up Learning and Teaching Centres to support IT based learning, or are in the process of doing so. For those who are successful, the prizes are potentially very great.

However, the threats are also very real. "How much income would our business schools lose if Harvard were to market MBAs globally on the Internet?" (Hodges, 1998). The opportunity to develop global education brands in all vocational sectors, including hospitality, has surely now arrived.

However, suppliers of Web-based learning are not limited to universities. Disney was the first corporation to set up its own "university". Body Shop followed with its New Academy of Business. In the hospitality sector, Marriott is involved in pilot activity towards setting up a Virtual University. There are signs that Business Schools are beginning to appreciate the growing economic and social importance of the hospitality industry.

They may become more involved, particularly in continuing professional development. The Henley Centre was the preferred contractor for the Joint Hospitality Industry Congress research into the future of the hospitality industry in the twenty-first century (Henley Centre, 1996). London Business School has also researched hotels as part of a study of service industry competitiveness (Voss *et al.*, 1997). Given this research interest, how long before the service sector and hospitality receive increasing attention in study programmes? This could be via traditional delivery or online.

Open University Business School and *Financial Times* Education could both be potentially very powerful online competitors. Amongst UK Hospitality Education Institutions, Oxford Brookes has been at the forefront of Web-based learning through its collaborative agreements with Online Education, Hong Kong and International Management Centres, UK. Under the terms of these agreements, Brookes controls the curriculum and quality, whilst the collaborative partners input technological and learning delivery expertise. Undoubtedly other hospitality education international suppliers will come on stream in the near future.

A further potential consequence of technologically based learning delivery is increased prominence being given to acknowledged experts in particular areas of the hospitality curriculum. Centres of expertise may be institutions or individual academics. As broad band capability develops, there is no reason why students should not enjoy access to lively and informed learning materials, produced by the very best in the international field.

As such learning resources develop, it is feasible that some educational centres will develop curriculum, whilst others focus on facilitating learning programmes based around them. In this way, the present diverse curriculum may become more standardised around acknowledged sources of expertise. As the new millennium approaches, there are important short-term issues which will demand the attention of education managers. Some of those which will concern UK providers have been discussed here. Whilst engaging with these, managers will also need to be aware of the potential for revolutionary change brought about by the advent of new learning technology. This is likely to fundamentally change international hospitality education very soon into the next millennium.

Merits

- Introduction. TQM as a slogan has been around since 1985. TQM provides a management system, using various combinations of tools that have been in existence for much longer. Each tool has its own use, with benefits that follow. TQM leads to a synergy of benefits.
- Through the application of TQM, senior management will empower all levels of management, including self management at worker level, to manage quality systems.
- Outlined below are some advantages to be gained by a hotel, from the use of TQM. These are split into the five key areas of TQM.
- Continuous Improvement. People wish to improve themselves and get a better lifestyle. If the desire for individual improvement is transferred to systems within the workplace, then these systems will improve.
- Management can, at times, be a restraint to innovation through relying on historical systems. This will result in "always do what you have always done and you will always get what you have always got".
- A good chef will know how best to prepare and present food. If given the freedom to innovate then

the standard of food will improve.

- When mistakes are made by staff, it is rarely through a desire to make a mistake. The system used is at fault. With departments constantly striving for improvement, hotel systems will improve, leading to reduced internal costs and a better service for customers.
- Multifunctional Teams. Within the hotel, departments are customers and suppliers for each other. A waiter is the chef's supplier giving information on what has been ordered from the menu including any special requests about how the food should be prepared (medium, well done etc). When the food is ready, the roles are reversed. The chef becomes the waiter's supplier providing the food.
- If the hotel's organisation is structured in such a way, that people in different departments work with each other to solve problems as a team, traditional inter departmental barriers will be removed. Inter departmental communication on a day to day basis is essential for effective management.
- Multifunctional teamwork allows the problems and requirements of each department to be passed on at worker level, throughout the hotel. This will lead to a better understanding of how the hotel systems work, by all employees.
- Individuals will work with each other identifying causes of problems rather than blaming each other for the results of a problem. This will remove the blame culture.
- Reduction in Variation. Systems are influenced by many elements which cause variation. For example, as new staff are employed, they will do their jobs in a different way to previous staff. This can lead to a change in the service provided by the hotel. If such

influences can be minimised, then standards of service can be maintained.

— This can be achieved by documenting systems. Giving workers the opportunity to own their processes by letting them do this documentation boosts morale. Also, the documentation will accurately reflect what is actually done rather than what management thinks is done. Initially this will lead to guests receiving a known standard of service which will result in repeat business.

— Once the standard is stabilised, changes made to improve the service can be measured and directly linked to the improvement made.

— Supplier Integration. By involving your suppliers directly with your staff, two way communication can be established. Your chef can explain the standard of food required. Your supplier can explain the difficulties in supplying such food. Any problems that arise can be solved jointly, using your knowledge of hotel systems, the chef's knowledge of food and the suppliers expertise in supply systems.

— This prevents waste through returned goods for the supplier. Expense through:

— Obtaining replacements from another supplier.

— A drop in service by not being able to provide what was intended.

— Education and Training. Through education, management and staff are given the tools to achieve all the above. Education provides for guided innovation from all levels. Training, which is a cost, shows a commitment by management to:

— Individual staff self improvement, which is a motivator.

— TQM.

— Staff will collectively provide continual improvement of hotel systems. By working together, communication/departmental barriers will be broken down. The standard of service can be set, maintained and then improved. Suppliers will be working with rather than working for the hotel. The standard of staff and management will improve through education. The adoption of a new attitude to work, by everyone embracing the ideas of TQM.

Quality Assurance

The quality assurance framework depicted and integrates the input, process and output elements of a hotel's operational system and takes an open system perspective where service quality and operational efficiencies work together rather than against each other. The framework stresses customer orientation as its guiding principle, and merges statistical and affordable computer technologies in delivery of high quality service to customers. The framework divides the operations system of a hotel into two subsystems: manufacturing and service subsystems. While having different characteristics, the two systems are highly interdependent. The overall effectiveness and efficiency of the entire operation is very much dependent on the synergies of the two subsystems and their abilities to contribute to the goals of the entire system. The nature, features and objectives of these two subsystems are discussed next.

The Manufacturing Subsystem

This subsystem represents the back-stage operations and activities of a hotel which, typically, are not directly observable by customers. It resembles the production operations system of a manufacturing organization and shares several of its characteristics. For instance, like a manufacturing operations system, the subsystem is responsible for the efficient performance of all operational tasks, which among others, include demand forecast, material acquisition and handling, staff scheduling, work-load determination and production planning. As in the case of a production operations system, this subsystem is also process driven and quality control charts such as the x bar, sigma and R charts are used to monitor various processes and to determine whether they are in or out of control. The overall objective of the quality assurance efforts is to ensure internal quality and adherence to process standards. To achieve these objectives, the subsystem relies on a user-friendly information system and related technologies in the forms of hardware, software, networks and databases.

It should, however, be noted that while many of the backstage activities are not directly observable by customers, any problems in their performance may have direct influence on customer satisfaction. For instance, understaffing due to poor work scheduling may translate into delays in cleaning the rooms and having them ready for customer check-in at promised times. This may be a cause of irritation for customers who are unaware of the "behind the scenes" problems and could result in dissatisfaction.

The Service Subsystem

This subsystem encompasses the "front-stage activities" in a hotel. Because these activities involve direct encounter with the service provider, customers are extremely concerned with the performance of the service subsystem. Each service encounter is as important as any other, and each and every one of them has to be managed well since customer satisfaction with these encounters ultimately affects their perception of service quality. The service subsystem is outcome driven and customer focused. Not only perceived quality but also consistency of service are of utmost significance. Customers expect the same level of service from all the staff all the time. Any inconsistencies in the chain of services provided by the luggage handlers, bill captain, receptionist, the cleaning staff, the hotel-shuttle driver, restaurant staff, etc. may not only irritate the customers but also magnify any negative perceptions they may have.

This chain is easily broken at its weakest point: one bad experience may destroy the image of the entire hotel. Functional rather than technical quality is of utmost concern in the service subsystem. For example, whether a clerk at the front desk is using the latest computer hardware and software are of little concern to the customer. What is important to the customer is the accuracy and efficiency of the reservation system. Hence, human, as opposed to technological approaches, are more critical in the service subsystem.

Service Quality

Managers in organizations in both public and private sectors face many challenges. Among these are the need to manage rapid changes in social values in the workplace, new practices, new technologies, etc., more productively and democratically. Research carried out by Comen, into hotel quality assurance programmes, highlighted the following points as common barriers to success in achieving total quality within the service industry: outside obstacles and those arising from the nature of the service industry, lack of commitment from management, lack of top management visibility, lack of financial or human resources, problem solving which was perceived to take too long, individuals becoming side-tracked in quality meetings, lack of non-member awareness and absenteeism and attrition.

According to Harwood and Pieters, successful management of organization-wide quality improvement effort must include three parts:

— A set of core concepts which provide common terminology and ideas about quality and its meaning and application to all individuals at work. These must be known and applied by all members of the organization.

— A systematic and common process that everyone uses for identifying and working quality issues through to effective prevention or corrective action.
— A set of managing elements which define the areas for change in an effective organizational change. Attention to the full set of elements is necessary to move quality improvement from a secondary position to a most important task and keep it that way.

In other words managers must:

— Organize themselves and others for dealing with quality issues. It is essential that all staff have a common definition of service quality and quality must be included as part of shortand long-term plans. Quality must be measured and individuals held responsible for improvement, i.e., make quality a primary factor in performance evaluations and rewards.
— Ensure that the customer is the main priority throughout the organization. Creating a customer-centred culture requires of management both a philosophical commitment and skilled training for implementation.

Given the apparent simplicity of the concept, it is justifiable to question why its potential was not fully recognizable sooner in the service sector of the British economy. The answer to that probably lies in the complexity of the business environment of today. It usually takes a major jolt to bring clarity and focus to the confusion of aims and objectives which characterize most businesses. Whatever the stimulus there are now numerous examples of companies which have used the concept to fight back against national and international competition successfully.

Assessment

Alongside the approach to learning and teaching and the

curriculum, other means of differentiating and positioning vocational education's offering to students and employers will also be important. Certainly in the run up to the millennium, hospitality education centres will be increasingly preoccupied with the forthcoming subject quality review. Reaching the Holy Grail of 24 points will be a prime objective for those who consider themselves to be front runners. Achieving at least a respectable performance will be important for all. Planning for success has been made more problematic by the existing arrangements being in force only until September 2000 (QAA, 1997). The hospitality review (along with leisure and tourism) is therefore on the cusp between the existing and the new system.

It now seems likely that the existing system will be the one used. Therefore the six review areas of: curriculum design, content and organisation; teaching, learning and assessment; student progression and achievement; student support and guidance; learning resources; and quality management and enhancement will all be receiving much attention during the next two years.

Quality and quality assessment are therefore inextricably entwined with the emerging debate on graduate descriptors. Centres will need to have a clear view of their educational aims and objectives. If the CHME line is followed, this will include achievement of both the general hospitality graduate descriptors, aspirations regarding the operational context and the units of National Vocational Standards which the learning outcomes are underpinning.

The link between centres' graduate aspirations and the quality assessment areas of curriculum design, content, learning and assessment and learning resources should therefore be able to be clearly articulated. A complication in planning for quality assessment will be caused by the international links which many centres have forged over the past few years. As would be expected from a vocational education sector which supports such an internationally oriented industry, these are extensive. Provision for quality assurance and control will need to demonstrate that international educational collaboration is planned and administered in a sound way which delivers consistently, even in remote satellite centres. The seriousness of the quality review is compounded by the fact that the results of assessment will stay with centres for at least five years. A high or poor score will have considerable impact on both recruitment and industry relations. Demonstrating that a centre is "quality approved" will surely have higher priority than any other educational management activity.

Quality and Customers

A summary of the articles on the themes of service quality and customers is provided. Through effective human resource management an organization can create an environment which encourages and rewards employees for providing quality service to guests. In order for this to occur, management must know what quality service entails and how it can be properly measured. Getty and Thompson conducted research geared towards creating a reliable and valid instrument to measure customers' perceptions of delivered quality.

In addition, Bojanic and Rosen used an instrument for measuring service quality SERVQUAL to examine the association between service quality as perceived by customers and its service determinants. Management attempts to measure service quality not only from the guest's perspective, but from the employee's as well. It is important for management to be able to quantify the interpersonal skills required by employees in service positions. In two separate studies, Samenfink utilized a self-monitoring scale to determine the theoretical characteristics required of employees to be successful in the service encounter. Once the service encounter is complete, attempts can be made to measure the customer's overall satisfaction. Barsky created his own definition of customer satisfaction along with a practical approach to facilitate its measurement. Almanza *et al.*, on the other hand, used Albrecht and Bradford's service attribute matrix to determine attributes leading to customer satisfaction.

All of these models, scales, and surveys used to measure service may seem redundant, but in order to provide quality service it is imperative to know what quality service is. How management defines quality service is insignificant; how the customer defines it is paramount. Once management is able to identify and provide quality service, the next step is to attempt to attract customers to serve. Measuring how a customer makes a choice between hospitality products is a bit more difficult than some of the other measurement methods previously discussed. The customer's choice of a hospitality product frequently involves trade-offs among multiattribute product alternatives, and a majority of the attributes, such as location, brand name, image, ambience, and amenities, are difficult if not impossible to measure quantifiably. Lewis *et al.* along with others, have used conjoint, or trade-off, analysis to measure customer's choice preferences.

Determining customer preferences is important to an organization's success. However, those of us in the hospitality industry must attract customers in the first place. Knowing who the customer is and how to reach him/her is therefore essential. The methods management use to reach its customers depend on the type of customer sought. Vogt *et al.*examine how meeting planners use personal sources of information, such as prior experience or the advice of others, when making their client's travel arrangements. Conversely, Mihalik *et al.* compared published sources of information used by Japanese and German international travellers when determining overseas vacation destinations.

In order to reach and attract customers successfully, management must also be aware of the prevailing dynamic socio-demographic characteristics. Francese warns that managers need to realize that the post-baby-boom hospitality consumers will be few in numbers, tough in spirit, pragmatic, and technologically aware. On the other hand, Lago and Poffley address the demographic variability among the elderly with respect to health status, income, and family structure. In either case, awareness of the differences between demographic groups can assist management in identifying the needs of individuals in those groups in order to provide them with quality service.

Implementing QM

The issues hospitality groups/hotels should consider when implementing a QM programme, from start to implementation. The inputs for this model were generated from the review of literature. The proposed model comprises of five stages. The five stages of the model include:

— awareness and commitment;
— planning;
— programming;
— implementing; and
— evaluation.

In the first phase of the model, the top management must develop a complete understanding of what is QM and how they plan to achieve it. Once the understanding and commitment is made, in the second phase of the model, the management should do the following: perform an internal quality assessment of the organization to identify strengths and weaknesses, provide education to key personnel (including physicians), set visions and objectives in writing, and design a new system. Hospitality managers should take care to ensure that the organization's culture is suitable to foster QM. Its culture has to agree with basic QM values and visions. In the third phase, the management should name the process; state purpose through a new quality framework; provide training to all levels of personnel; conduct internal and external customer surveys to evaluate the current process and make necessary adjustments; formulate a quality council to oversee and regulate the QM process; perform competitive benchmarking to compare its performance to other organizations; form quality improvement teams; and establish measures and quality indicators which truly measure the objectives and goals of the organization.

When naming the process, every effort should be made to disassociate QM in the hospitality industry with QM in other industries, since medical employees view themselves as different from manufacturing employees. The fourth phase, referred to as "implementation" should involve providing ongoing education and training; forming new committees, new teams, new departments or hiring new specialists to help the process as and when required; and recognizing and rewarding quality improvements. Recognition can be a valuable tool in improving employee morale, self-interest, and interest in QM. The reward system, however, must be managed carefully. The final phase of the model should involve evaluating success or failure of the QM programme. This should be conducted annually. For example, if the programme is not achieving its goals, it should be redesigned.

Necessary Steps and Factors

To ensure successful implementation of a quality assurance system as outlined in the preceding section certain steps are in order. First, while many informed observers of the hospitality industry have advocated divergent perspectives on service quality and quality assurance, they all agree that the success of a quality assurance system depends on an organizational culture that fosters and facilitates service quality (Clark, 1984; Glover *et al.*, 1984; Pickworth, 1987).

For example, the Stouffer Hotel chain, which has a successful quality assurance programme, prides itself on its organizational culture motivated by the broad vision "We intend to be the place to stay, the place to work and the place to invest" (Bohan and Horney, 1991). Without a doubt, top management's commitment to service quality and quality assurance is vital to the success of any quality assurance programme (Comen, 1989) as demonstrated by the experience of the Roadway Inns (*Lodging Hospitality*, 1982). Second, an audit of entire operations is needed to determine whether various organizational strategies are in harmony or not. In carrying out this audit, the assistance of external experts should be sought.

Third, given the tremendous importance of service provider-customer interaction in the hospitality industry, hiring the right people, and then training and rewarding them for quality performance are crucial (Breen, 1985; Hesser, 1988; Horak, 1991; Selwitz, 1992). To guide the selection of the right people, job descriptions should be examined critically and, wherever necessary, be modified with a view to promote customer orientation. Training of employees should not be geared only at skills-training. Through role-playing and sensitivity training techniques, employees also must be taught how to handle delicate encounters and how to deal with the frustrations and stresses of their jobs.

It is likewise important to get the employees involved in quality assurance efforts by soliciting their concerns, opinions and suggestions. For instance, via the "Bright Idea Programme", the management of the Captain Cook Hotel not only encourages employees to provide suggestions but also seeks their input in setting the standards for various tasks performed at the hotel (*Lodging Hospitality*, 1987). Employee involvement is vital in identifying problems as seen by employees and motivating them towards solutions. Fourth, an audit of back-stage (i.e. the manufacturing subsystem) operations should be undertaken. A multifaceted analysis should aim at establishing performance standards for tasks related to the back-stage operations. In setting the standards, besides employees, industry experts should be used. The standards should be clear, realistic and firm.

In addition, the standards should be consistent with the overall organizational culture. Fifth, technologies used should be examined critically to determine whether they are state-of-the-art and/or how much new investment is needed to update them. This is imperative at a time when the automation wave revolutionizing various aspects of hotel operations including reservations systems, environmental control systems and security systems all of which are critical for operational efficiency and customer orientation. Sixth, current channels and flow of information and feedback mechanisms should be scrutinized carefully.

This may reveal areas where modifications are needed and enable the management to make the necessary operational and strategic adjustments. Seventh, the relationship between the organization and its main suppliers should be analysed thoroughly. Establishment of just-in-time (JIT) and total quality management (TQM) programmes with suppliers may indeed enhance both operational and strategic efficiency and effectiveness. Eighth, the feasibility of incorporating quantitative tools such as waiting line models, demand forecasting models, scheduling techniques, quality control procedures and inventory models into existing operations should be investigated. Ninth, to assess current levels of customer satisfaction with service quality and to ascertain their expectations, customer surveys and focus group interviews should be conducted. Such surveys should be complemented by direct observations of customers while they interact with the service providers.

As a closing note it should be reiterated that the success of a quality assurance programme depends on commitment to customers, commitment to excellence, team work and, above all top management enthusiasm. This means top executives should take the lead to create an organizational culture which is conducive to the success of a quality assurance programme and must champion efforts in that direction.

Research Assessment

Hospitality has recently emerged as a strongly developing research area. Over the past five years, both quantity and quality of research activity have made considerable progress. Consequently performance in research will also be a very pressing concern in the run up to the next Research Assessment Exercise (RAE) in 2001. However, there remain very considerable obstacles to gaining a clear picture of how hospitality management research is actually performing across individual Higher Education Institutions.

The Units of Assessment (UOAs) for the forthcoming research assessment will remain the same as the last one in 1996 (HEFC, 1998). This means that hospitality research may be submitted in two major categories; both Unit 43, Business and Management (covering the full range of related single and multi disciplinary research including hospitality management and tourism) and Unit 69, Sports Related Subjects (including physical education, sport science, leisure, recreation and sports studies) will have a hospitality sub-panel. Additionally, catering is also included in Unit 16, Food Science and Technology. In the previous RAE, hospitality related research was also submitted under other UOAs, for example Unit 21 Environmental Studies.

The multiple options open for the assessment of hospitality research reflects the varied organisational contexts in which hospitality management is located within UK universities. It has already been noted that hospitality management is a "small and distinctive" area of higher educational activity, located within various departments, schools, and faculties. Often this is alongside other areas of study such as food, tourism and leisure, which are considered to be related by the host institution. The impact of this diversity in approach is that the major research players will be assessed in different UOAs, i.e. different playing fields. Whilst CHME may have a view as to where it may prefer hospitality research to be assessed, the reality of the situation is that it is the individual institutions where submission decisions are taken.

These will reflect the institutions' best interests. They will take full advantage of the flexibility which is available. A less than clear situation will be made even more opaque by the ability of hospitality management research to "piggy back" on the efforts of other research areas, rather than being assessed separately.

Examples at the 1996 RAE included hospitality's inclusion as an intrinsic part of business school and leisure submissions, where the wider area of research activity was particularly strong. In many institutions hospitality was therefore in a position to gain from the kudos of a considerably higher rating than was deserved by its own research performance. Some schools have been quick to take advantage of these "piggy back" ratings in publicity materials, even though many would argue that they are very misleading. The situation will be equally unsatisfactory in 2001. The research performance in hospitality management will continue to be very opaque. Whilst departments such as Hotel and Restaurant Management at Oxford Brookes University have decided to submit in their own right, most major institutions involved in hospitality research will receive ratings which are at least partially the result of other disciplines' efforts.

Undoubtedly out of all this confusion and lack of clarity, some prominent research players are likely to emerge. If hospitality management research has indeed moved forward, then following the 2001 RAE it should be in a position to gain greater financial resources from the overall research funds which host institutions receive. In the new millennium, this will bring about a further notch-up in research activity in the hospitality area, but concentrated in particular research oriented institutions, rather than across the board.

TQM and Environmental Change

This sub-theme looks at the impact the environment has on industry segments and markets. Harnson claims that the restaurant sector operates in a rapidly changing environment and, because of this, restaurant operators cope with change. Using the restaurant sector and other examples Harrison provides a framework for managing change. Muller and Woods provide an analysis of restaurant failures over a ten-year period in three different markets. They state "while generally attributed to operator mismanagement, [failure] may rely more on environmental conditions than individual management practices". The authors imply that good management may not always be able to overcome negative environmental conditions. Parsa and Khan look at how environmental changes have affected the quick service food sector. Chon and Huo provide an environmental analysis of the conference centre business. Welsh and Swerdlow look at how the globalization of business and the fall of the Soviet Union have created opportunities for the hospitality industry in the Russian Federation.

This sub-theme investigates specific issues that have developed because of changes in the business environment. A hotel tax on room sales is often seen by local politicians as a way to raise taxes from visitors and lessen the burden on the local population, the voters. Ahmed and Krohn examine the impact of hotel taxes in cities across the USA. Most studies show that a small increase has little impact on demand; however, in New York a percentage tax in double digits was found to have a negative impact on demand. The authors cite one study that found that tourists were more price sensitive than was previously realized. Ahmed and Krohn take the position that a small tax, where the proceeds are used to benefit the tourist industry, can be useful.

However, they caution that the hospitality industry must monitor the tax legislation to make sure the proceeds will benefit the tourist industry. Myers and Urdang discuss a change in the legal environment, lender liability, and the implications of this change for the hospitality industry. The authors state that senior management should be aware that in certain circumstances lenders can be held legally responsible to third parties for the wrongful act or omissions of the borrower. Jaffe *et al.* state that the USA is one of the leading producers of solid waste in the world. Landfills for this waste are quickly disappearing, resulting in the disposal of solid waste being ranked as one the most important environmental problems faced by public and private decision makers. The authors research current practices and provide recommendations for managers. Gaston reports on the implications of a recent court case involving trade-dress in the restaurant sector.

The concept of total quality management in service industries is still evolving. Vladimir investigates how quality is achieved on one of the top rated cruise lines, Seabourn. Breiter and Fried-Kline cite the lack of research on what hotels are actually accomplishing in terms of total quality management as one of the justifications for their study. In their study the authors investigate and report on the best practices of the hotels in the USA known for their total quality management systems.

The fourth sub-theme is strategy. Only one article was published on overall strategy during this six-year period. Haywood puts forth ten principles of strategy that corporate strategists could utilize in testing their strategic theories, concepts and plans.

Quality Systems

The organisational structure, responsibilities, procedures, processes and resources for implementing quality management. Key terms in quality management related to HRM:

(i) *Quality Assurance:* methods and systems for ensuring that products, services, facilities, policies, procedures and practices reach the same level of requirement

(ii) *Quality Systems',* methods which underpin and provide for the delivery of quality

(iii) *RS5750:* the UK standard for quality assurance systems

(iv) *Investors in People:* Government initiative aimed at improving organisations' investment, training and development of its employees

(v) *HACCP (Hazard Analysis Critical Control Point):* a

system related to the monitoring and management of approaches and methods related to the production of food

(vi) *Total Quality Management (TQM):* an approach to quality management which encompasses a variety of tools centring on the philosophy that the organisation can only develop with the involvement and commitment of all employees

Overall there exists two types of development in Quality Management, both of which will affect the management of people in the future.

1. Functional Systems and Approaches

These concentrate on processes, systems, written documentation and procedures to enforce a quality management approach on the organisation and its employees. Additionally, this area could include 'Investors in People' (IIP) which, whilst a developmental approach, does rely heavily on functional systems, policies and procedures. An example would be BS5750.

2. Conceptual Approaches

These concentrate on the development of organisational culture via people, to maintain and improve quality. Such approaches, whilst in part paper based, rely heavily on the involvement of all employees in quality improvement. TQM is an example of this.

Value Strategy

Managers when reexamining their existing service offering also need to decide which innovations will create value. For example, managers must ask themselves, which innovations not only deliver additional value to their customers but also are economically viable to the firm. Customer value can be defined as, "the customer's perception of what they want to have happen in a specific-use situation, with the help of a product and service offering in order to accomplish a desired purpose or goal". (*Stahl et al.*). The hospitality industry has an abundance of options which to choose from, when determining which products and services will add value for their customers. For example, a hotel operator can offer various combinations of traditional value drivers such as price, location, and typical hotel amenities, such as pool or work-out facilities. On the other hand, new and innovative value drivers could be offered which include features such as online reservations, in-room high-speed internet access, customization of room décor, and flexible check in/out policies. Before introducing a new service innovation, hotel managers need to assess the value that it will bring to their customers. A good understanding of value can be gained through empirical research methods, such as customer surveys.

Survey research relies heavily on a customer's perception of the functionality, performance, and worth of a supplier's offerings (*Anderson and Narus*). By acquiring the vital information of why guests choose to stay at particular hotels, hotel managers are better able to understand the attributes which drive guest's purchasing decisions. Furthermore, understanding the guest's needs and desires is invaluable when determining methods for improving company image. A lack of customer preference understanding leads to problems in both product and service design (*Schall*). Research shows that the most successful companies are the ones which are fully aware of customer preferences and develop their services in line with targeted market needs (*Karmarkar*).

As a competing service firm, it is essential to not only consider the types of innovative attributes to offer but also which operational strategy must be implemented to achieve the firm's goals. *Kim and Mauborgne* coined the term "value innovative logic" which differs from a more conventional approach. The conventional objective is to maximize the value of industrial bound offerings while the value innovative goal is to aid the innovative aspect of the service offering (*Kim and Mauborgne*).

Our research focuses on the value innovation logic for product and service offerings. Therefore, rather than taking a more traditional approach in determining which product and services to offer, an innovative logic approach presents options, "... in terms of the total solution customers seek, even if that takes the company beyond its industry's traditional offerings".

Customer Service Improvements

CRMs are claimed to improve customer service. Proponents say they can improve customer service by facilitating communication in several ways:

- Provide product information, product use information, and technical assistance on web sites that are accessible 24 hours a day, 7 days a week
- Help to identify potential problems quickly, before they occur
- Provide a user-friendly mechanism for registering customer complaints (complaints that are not registered with the company cannot be resolved, and are a major source of customer dissatisfaction)
- Provide a fast mechanism for handling problems and complaints (complaints that are resolved quickly can increase customer satisfaction)
- Provide a fast mechanism for correcting service deficiencies (correct the problem before other customers experience the same dissatisfaction)
- Identify how each individual customer defines quality, and then design a service strategy for each customer

based on these individual requirements and expectations

- use internet cookies to track customer interests and personalize product offerings accordingly
- use the internet to engage in collaborative customization or real-time customization
- Provide a fast mechanism for managing and scheduling followup sales calls to assess post-purchase cognitive dissonance, repurchase probabilities, repurchase times, and repurchase frequencies
- Provide a fast mechanism for managing and scheduling maintenance, repair, and on-going support (improve efficiency and effectiveness)
- Provide a mechanism to track all points of contact between a customer and the company, and do it in an integrated way so that all sources and types of contact are included, and all users of the system see the same view of the customer (reduces confusion)
- The CRM can be integrated into other cross-functional systems and thereby provide accounting and production information to customers when they want it.

Customer Choices

Customers, in a number of industries, are constantly bombarded with run-of-the-mill product and service offerings. As a result, customers both desire and more often demand innovative alternatives. In response, many service-oriented firms are striving to integrate novel features into their product-service offerings. Even product-oriented firms have noted the benefits of adding service innovation to their business strategies. For example, during recent years, IBM, a predominantly product-oriented firm, generated over half of its total revenue from services. Yet, only 15 percent of IBM's research and development budget was being allocated to services (Fitzgerald, 2005). Realizing this discrepancy, IBM recently realigned its strategy and business plan emphasizing service-based innovations. The new strategy was a resounding success. With one of IBM's innovative service programs adding over $300 million to last year's total revenue (Fitzgerald, 2005).

The benefits of service innovation are apparent. What is not as clear is how managers should decide on which innovations to implement. In some cases, innovative service offerings are necessary just to maintain a firm's current market share. This phenomenon suggests "... that some innovations may merely raise the cost of doing business without a significant economic benefit, other than to preserve current business and without providing a competitive edge... " (*Reid and Sandler*). However, other innovations may enhance service differentiation and induce financial gains. Thus, it is important for managers to implement innovations which are not only desired by customers but also are economically beneficial to the firm (*Reid and Sandler*).

Hospitality firms, such as hotels, are an ideal example of a market which could benefit from the implementation of service innovation. First, from a customer's perspective, the hospitality market is perpetually inundated by many similar, often easily substitutable service offerings. This can cause difficulties for hotel managers as they attempt to differentiate an individual hotel from its competitors (*Reid and Sandler*).

One solution to this challenge may be to offer new and innovative features to customers. Secondly, the hospitality industry is rapidly changing due to accelerations in information technology (*Olsen and Connolly*). Managers will need to make proactive changes which focus even more intensely on customer preferences, quality, and technological interfaces in order to stay competitive in such a dynamic environment (*Karmarkar*). Thirdly, travelers today do not exhibit, as in past decades, a truly brand loyal behavior. Travelers instead are choosing to patronize hotels that offer the best value proposition under existing budgetary constraints. (*Olsen and Connolly*). In order to add value to the guests' experience, hotel managers and marketers must meet the challenge of determining which services are preferred by hotel guests (*Olsen and Connolly*). Once a manager understands customers' preferences, the challenge then becomes prioritizing those preferences which add the greatest value to the hotel's existing service offering.

The purpose of this study is to explore customer tradeoffs for service innovation. The paper will examine the addition of innovative offerings and its relation to the hotel's core service concept. The service concept encompasses both the "how", in other words, the operations content, and the "what", the marketing content, of service design as well as the integration of the two (*Goldstein et al.*). In other words, we will examine the innovative service preferences of hotel guests, while also exploring how these preferences align with the strategic intent of the firm. Aligning customer preferences with operational strategy is important because operational constraints make it impossible to implement all options of innovative service offerings. Instead, hotel managers need to develop an understanding of market preferences prior to the addition of new services. This type of knowledge will enable managers to select innovative offerings that are most beneficial to the firm and that will truly have an impact on customer's choices.

The importance of studying innovation's role in services seems obvious. Yet, analysis in service innovation research is lacking in comparison to product innovation research (*Chesbrough*). Research which examines the opportunities and risks specific to service innovation as well as the choice sets for system design is needed to further the knowledge in service innovation research (*Chesbrough*). In this paper, we provide insight into service innovation by exploring the hotel preferences of both business and leisure travelers. We specifically aim to:

— Understand the trade-offs made for business and leisure travelers when choosing a hotel, in terms of innovative hotel market drivers or attributes.
— Explore the influence the addition of innovative services has on the design of the core service concept.
— Examine the impact of innovative service preferences on operational strategy formulation.

We believe that achieving these objectives will be beneficial to academics and practitioners when considering the impact service innovation has on a given firm's core concept. The structure of the paper is organized in the following manner: first, we give a general overview of the previous research regarding the service concept and innovation value. Next we discuss the current hotel innovations that pertain to our study. We then describe our research methods and the application of discrete choice modeling. In addition, we discuss the tradeoffs made by business and leisure travelers when selecting a hotel. We conclude by providing insights into service concept development as well as operational strategy formulation.

The wide array of research related to service innovation has primarily focused on the definition of the "service concept" (Goldstein *et al.*, 2002). *Edvardsson and Olsson* defined the service concept as a "prototype for service, covering the needs of the customer and the design of the service". Previous research has discussed the critical role of the service concept in service design and development (*Edvardsson and Olsson*). Furthermore, Goldstein *et al.* (2002) propose that the service concept is the missing key element in service design research. They suggest that the service concept integrates the "how" and "what" of service design while keeping both the customers' needs and strategic intent of the firm in mind. In other words, the service concept gives a detailed description of what the customer needs and how the organization will deliver the service. The conceptual background of the "service concept" in operations management literature is similar to "marketing concept". The marketing concept is the key to achieving organizational goals and involves "... determining the needs and wants of target markets and delivering the desired (customer) satisfactions more effectively than competitors... " (*Agarwal et al.*). Firms that are considered to be market-oriented are presumed to have the capability of understanding their customers better than their competitors. Innovation plays an important role in the marketing concept because it gives the service firm the ability to stay ahead of its competitors through new market offerings. The association between innovation and the market-orientation of a firm was determined to be both positive and significant (*Agarwal et al.*). In other words, a more market-oriented firm is more likely to consider innovation, which ultimately leads to superior firm performance (*Agarwal et al., ; Han et al.*). The relationship found between innovation and market orientation emphasizes the importance of identifying customers' needs. By understanding customer tradeoffs, service firms will have a better market orientation with a resulting improvement in firm performance.

HRM: Quality Management

There is no doubting that HRM specialists recognise the need to incorporate Quality Management approaches into their systems; what will be interesting is how far these developments will affect organisations in the future. For the hospitality industry, with its increasing customer focus and customer orientation, the relevance of such methods can be easily identified. However, as the industry will remain dominated by small independent operations, the uptake of such methods may be concentrated on the medium to large companies. Certainly the cost of creating a BS5750 system of moving towards IIP is prohibitive for smaller employers. Regardless of its benefits, the costs of developing and installing Quality Management systems within an organisation will be too high for many hospitality operators. Such businesses will continue to rely on the skills and experience of owners and managers to maintain quality through basic people management approaches. Obviously, any change to operational strategy and approach will have effects on the management of people within an organisation. The personnel and human resource specialist will rightly be concerned with changes which impinge directly on the HR function. Systems such as BS5750, HACCP and IIP will affect policies and procedures related to:

(i) recruitment and selection
(ii) employee working conditions and benefits
(iii) employee communication
(iv) training and development

Approaches such as TQM (and in part IIP) will affect the manner in which the organisation communicates to, involves and empowers its employees and, therefore, has more to do with culture and approach than systems and procedures.

Overall, the trend has and will be to identify approaches that concentrate on the involvement and development of people, rather than the more functional based systems. This will result in personnel and human resource specialists increasingly being involved in the following activities:

(i) assisting the move towards people-based business strategies
(ii) facilitating increased involvement and empowerment of staff
(iii) designing 'systems' which help line managers and supervisors manage, motivate and encourage their stall'

(iv) more closely linking people development to business strategy and objectives

(v) developing improved lines of communication between all staff

(vi) concentrating more on the internal customers of an organisation, i.e. the individuals and teams who make up a company's workforce

Such activities will also involve changes in the future to employment practices and policies including:

(i) growth of more flexible employment and benefits packages

(ii) improvements in equality of opportunity

(iii) minor increase in alternative payment and reward systems, including:

(iv) *team based pay*, where small teams of employees are rewarded on the quality of performance and output of the whole team

(v) *individual performance related pay*, where an individual's pay (and potential increase or bonus) is based on the individual's achievement in terms of 'quality'.

(vi) *standards achievement pay*, where newly appointed employees' pay levels are set against the individual achievement of laid down standards of competence and quality

Increasing numbers of hospitality companies are developing pay and benefits packages which relate individual pay to the achievement of agreed standards and the demonstration of competence.

(i) involvement of employee in both personal and organisational development—employers will increasingly recognise that by assisting and encouraging individual employees to improve, the

> organisation itself will improve. As one director reported 'the quality of the business is dependent upon the quality and involvement of each of its employees'.

Quality management, then, is both a system and an approach and it is an element of HRM that will remain a central focus for hospitality operators over the next decade.

Challenges of Competitiveness

The research in the area of market sensitivity and competitiveness tended to be on yield management and positioning. The yield management research was grouped into two general issues, pricing systems to increase yield and the choice of market segments that would create the highest yield. The positioning articles discussed the use of perceptual maps as a strategic tool. The methodology used in the positioning articles could be applied to most hospitality companies, giving good information for strategic planning.

Yield Management

The yield management articles are broken up into conventional yield management articles and methods for choosing the market segments that will create the highest yield. Griffin (1995) provided an overview of yield management and identified a number of critical success factors for yield management systems. Among these are several environmental factors that relate to booking patterns, price sensitivity of market segments, and the distribution channel's tolerance for differential pricing.

Jeffrey and Hubbard (1994) developed a model of occupancy performance that can be easily applied by hotel managers and others with access to hotel occupancy data. The model looked at two fundamental aspects of a hotel's occupancy performance: the proportionality component, which includes the effects of regular and periodic demand fluctuations, and the competitive components, which include local and unique forces. Bull (1994) investigated the contribution a hotel's location makes to the market value of the hotel's rooms.

This methodology makes it possible to put implicit price-location contours on an area map. The study also has implications for area growth that may affect the contribution of a property's location to its room rate. Weatherford (1995) cited the importance of incorporating a guest's length of stay into the room allocation decisions. He claimed proper use of the length of stay dimension can increase revenue by up to 3 per cent.

One of the problems with most yield management systems is that they only look at room revenue. Quain (1992) introduced profit analysis by segment (PABS). PABS takes into account room and non-room revenue to determine the value of different market segments. As yield management matures in the hotel industry, more robust models will be developed that take into account total guest expenditures and the long-term value of the guest. In developing yield management systems it is important that customer retention be included in the model. Maximizing revenue today has little value if it drives off tomorrow's customers.

Positioning/perceptual Maps

Dev *et al.* (1995) cited the need for managers to monitor the implications of their marketing strategies. The authors stated that managers need to examine the attributes that consumers use to differentiate one hotel brand from another and illustrated how managers can do this by using multidimensional scaling to build perceptual maps.

Kim (1996) used perceptual maps to show how customers perceive food and beverage at competing hotels. Kim also developed ideal points to show how a hotel can change its attributes to gain a better position *vis-à-vis* its competitors. The methodology used in the study could be used to position different product or product groups of a hotel or restaurant. Shaw (1992) investigated price from a strategic positioning viewpoint. She explained how price has both a strategic component and a tactical component. Shaw stated a positioning approach focuses first on price levels, then on actual price decisions for a specific product. Shaw's approach to pricing could help a brand achieve a desired position, which then could be validated through one of the perceptual mapping techniques.

Glossary

Attendance Building. Marketing and promotional programs designed to increase attendance at conventions, trade shows, meetings, and events.

Attraction. Any visitor service or product which tourists would enjoy visiting or using. An attraction may not be an "attractor" but can still be an attraction. To be considered an attraction, a product must be: A. Findable (clearly located on maps and street addresses, and directions provided). If tourists can't find the facility, it is not a tourist attraction. B. Hours of operation clearly denoted in any and all promotional materials (if a tourist arrives only to find the attraction closed, it is not an attraction). Examples of attractions include everything from a theme park that attracts over a million visitors a year, to a produce stand by the side of the road. General all-inclusive term travel industry marketers use to refer to products that have visitor appeal, like museums, historic sites, performing arts institutions, preservation districts, theme parks, entertainment and national sites.

Attractor. A significant tourist attraction, which compels visitation. The primary "must sees" in an area. The top reasons a tourist would choose to visit this area.

Bed Tax. City or county tax added to the price of a hotel room.

Benchmarking. The process of comparing performance and processes within an industry to assess relative position against either a set industry standard or against those who are "best in class" (Synergy, 2000).

Best Practice(s). A term used to designate highest quality, excellence, or superior practices in a particular field by a tourism operator.

Blocked rooms. Hotel rooms held without a deposit.

Blocked. (1) Hotel rooms held without deposit. (2) Hotel rooms, airline tickets or other travel services held for a specific client.

Booking. Term used to refer to a completed sale by a destination, convention center, facility, hotel or supplier (i.e. convention, meeting, trade show or group business booking).

Brigade. French term used to describe all the staff working on the floor of the restaurant or the kitchen.

Business Travel. Travel for commercial, governmental or educational purposes with leisure as a secondary motivation.

Buyer. A member of the travel trade who reserves room blocks from accommodations or coordinates the development of a travel product.

BYO. Bring Your Own. A restaurant which allows patrons to bring their own alcohol.

Carrier. Any provider of mass transportation, usually used in reference to an airline.

Chambers of Commerce. Typically, a Chamber of Commerce will specialize in local economic development that can include tourism promotion.

Charter Group. Group travel in which a previously organized group travels together, usually on a custom itinerary.

Commissions. A percent of the total product cost paid to travel agents and other travel product distributors for selling the product to the consumer.

Consumer Show. A product showcase for the general public. Differs from a "Trade Show" as a trade show generally targets industry professionals. Consumer Shows target the consumer. Often there is a charge to get into the show.

Convention and Visitors Bureau. These organizations are local tourism marketing organizations specializing in developing conventions, meetings, conferences and visitations to a city, county or region.

Conventions and Trade Shows. Major segment of travel industry business. Trade shows differ from conventions in that they have exhibit space that provides product exhibition and sales opportunities for suppliers, as well as information gathering and buying opportunities for customers.

Conversion Study. Research study to analyze whether advertising respondents actually were converted to travelers as a result of advertising and follow-up material.

Co-op Advertising. Advertising funded by two or more destinations and /or suppliers.

Cooperative Marketing. Marketing programs involving two or more participating companies, institutions or organizations.

Cooperative Partner. An independent firm or organization which works with a tourism office by providing cash or in-kind contributions to expand the marketing impact of the tourism officeÕs program.

Country of Residence. Consists of the country where she/he has lived for most of the past year (12 months), or for a shorter period if she/he intends to return within 12 months to live there.

Cover. Each diner at a restaurant.

CRS. Central Reservation System

CTRLA. Car and Truck Rental and Leasing Association.

Cultural tourism. Travel for the purpose of learning about cultures or aspects of cultures (NEAP, 2000).

CVB. Convention and Visitors Bureau.

Day visitors. Visitors who arrive and leave the same day for leisure, recreation and holidays, visiting friends and relatives, & business and professional.

Destination Marketing Organization (DMO). A company or other entity involved in the business of increasing tourism to a destination or improving its public image. Local tourism marketing organizations, such as convention and visitors bureaus or chambers of commerce.

Destination Marketing. Marketing a city, state, country, area or region to consumers and trade.

Destination. A hotel, resort, attraction, city, region, or state.

Discounted Fare. Negotiated air fare for convention, trade show, meeting, group and corporate travel.

Discover America. Theme used by the Travel Industry Association and its marketing partners to market travel within the United States.

Ecotourism. "Responsible travel to natural areas that conserves the environment and improves the welfare of local people," according to The International Ecotourism Society.

Fam Tours. Organized trips for travel agents, tour operators, tour wholesalers or other members of the travel trade for the purpose of educating and "familiarizing" them with tourism destinations. By seeing the destinations where they are sending travelers, the travel trade is better prepared to answer customer questions and promote travel to the location. Also called "fams" or "familiarization tours."

Familiarization Trip. A complimentary or reduced-rate travel program for travel agents, airline or rail employees or other travel buyers, designed to acquaint participants with specific destinations or suppliers and to stimulate the sale of travel. Familiarization tours, also called fam tours, are sometimes offered to journalists as research trips for the purpose of cultivating media coverage of specific travel products.

Feeder Airport/City. An outlying city which feeds travelers to hubs or gateway cities.

FIT (Free Independent Travel). Individual travel in which a tour operator has previously arranged blocks of rooms at various destinations in advance for use by individual travelers. These travelers travel independently, not in a group, usually by rental car or public transportation.

Foreign Independent Travel or Foreign Individual Travel (FIT). An international pre-paid unescorted tour that includes several travel elements such as accommodations, rental cars and sightseeing. A FIT operator specialises in preparing FITs documents at the request of retail travel agents. FITs usually receive travel vouchers to present to on-site services as verification of pre-payment.

Frequency. The number of times an advertisement appears during a given campaign.

Fulfillment. Servicing consumers and trade who request information as a result of advertising or promotional programs. Service often includes an 800 number, sales staff and distribution of materials.

Function. Term used to for specialty catering such as weddings, meetings, birthdays, dances and product launches etc.

Gateway or Gateway City. A major airport, seaport, rail or bus center through which tourists and travelers enter from outside the region.

GDS. Global Distribution System, such as Sabre and Worldspan

GIT (Groups Independent Travel). Group travel in which individuals purchase a group package in which they will travel with others along a pre-set itinerary.

Gourmet. French term, originally and still used to describe a person who is a critic of food and beverage. Also used to describe establishments that provide sophisticated food and beverage.

Gross lettings. This refers to all room lettings, i.e. both paid & complimentary listings are included

Group Rate. Negotiated hotel rate for convention, trade show, meeting, tour or incentive group.

Group Tour and Group Leader - Group Tour. A travel agent type company which plans motor coach trips. Group Leader: A small, informal group, such as a church group, scout troop, or social group. Usually one person plans the activities for the group. Some travel shows target these planners such as GLAMER.

Head in Beds. Industry slang referring to the primary marketing objective of accommodations and most destinations. increasing the number of overnight stays.

Hospitality Industry. Another term for the travel industry.

Hospitality. A general term used in travel & tourism describing the "hospitality industry"; Refers to the general greeting, welcoming, food service, etc

Hotel Package. A package offered by a hotel, sometimes consisting of no more than a room and breakfast; sometimes, especially at resort hotels, consisting of (ground) transportation, rooms, meals, sports facilities and other components.

Hub and Spoke. Air carriers use of selected cities as "hubs" or connected points for service on their systems to regional destinations.

Hub. An airport or city which serves as a central connecting point for aircraft, trains or buses from outlying feeder airports or cities.

Icon. A facility or landmark which is visually synonymous with a destination.

IDS. Internet Distribution System

Incentive Tour. A trip offered as a prize, usually by a company to stimulate employee sales or productivity.

Incentive Travel. Travel offered as a reward for top performance and the business that develops, markets and operates these programs.

Inclusive Tour. A tour program that includes a variety of feature for a single rate (airfare, accommodations, sightseeing, performances, etc.)

Inquiry. A request for more information about an attraction or destination.

International Marketing. Marketing a destination, product or service to consumers and the trade outside the of the United States.

IPU. Interface Processing Unit

Itinerary. A travel schedule provided by a travel agent for his/her customer. A proposed or preliminary itinerary may be rather vague or specific. A final itinerary however provides all details (flight numbers, departure times, reservation confirmation numbers) and describes planned activities.

Joint venture. A form of strategic alliance or co-operative arrangement where ownership is shared and a separate enterprise formed. This may strengthen existing businesses through shared expertise, capital, removal of competition and creation of economies of scale. International tourism joint ventures between foreign organisations and local partners facilitate introduction of foreign products into local markets.

Jungle tourism. Jungle tours have become a major component of green tourism in tropical destinations. A jungle is a subclimax tropical forest consisting of a tangled growth of lianas, trees and scrub which may form an almost impenetrable barrier to the tourist. Jungle tours are a relatively recent phenomenon of Western international tourism.

Key-informant Survey. This involves interviewing people who are likely to have some insight into a problem: operating managers; sales staff; managers; suppliers; and consultants.

Keying. A social convention by which social 'reality' is transformed and seen as something else, such as the presentation of a fight as mere horseplay. In tourism, a peculiar, inverted variety of keying is frequently employed: the 'as if' situation in which participants are induced to playfully make believe that presented settings, activities or events are 'real', when as tourists they may be well aware that such occurences are contrived.

Leisure Tourist. Leisure tourists, in contrast with business travellers, travel for pleasure and thus are not under any obligations to frequent specific destinations or facilities. They tend to be price and fashion conscious, concentrate their touristic activities to specific (vacation) times, and are influenced by marketing and publicity. Leisure tourism is heavily influenced by living standards, discretionary income levels and vacation entitlements.

Leisure Travel. Travel for recreational, educational, sightseeing, relaxing and other experiential purposes.

Length of Stay. This refers to the period of time which people spend in a destination. Many definitions require that visitors to a destination stay at least 24 hours or overnight, and less than one year, to be considered a tourist. Destination areas often look for means to extend tourists' length of stay in order to increase positive economic impacts.

Limited Bar. Restricted service of alcoholic beverages at a function. For example, $1000 limit for beer, wine and soft drinks, or unlimited beer wine and soft drinks for four hours. In both cases spirits would incur additional costs.

Market Share. The percentage of business within a market category.

Market Volume. The total number of travelers within a market category.

Maximum Room Nights. This is calculated based on the total room inventory for all gazetted hotels.

Mise en place. Literally this means to 'put in place' and generally refers to pre-service preparation, including setting the tables and stocking up the stations. Also used in the kitchen, where it refers to the pre-preparation before cooking takes place.

Mission (Sales). A promotional and sales trip coordinated by a state travel office, conventional and visitors bureau or key industry member to increase product awareness, sales and to enhance image. Target audiences may include tour operators, wholesales, incentive travel planners, travel agents, meeting planners, convention and trade show managers and media. Missions often cover several international or domestic destinations and include private and public sector participants. Mission components can include receptions, entertainment representatives of the destination, presentations and pre- scheduled sales and media calls.

Motorcoach. Deluxe equipment used by most tour operators in group tour programs. Amenities include reclining seats, bathrooms, air conditioning, good lighting and refreshment availability.

Nature Tourism. Travel to unspoiled places to experience and enjoy nature.

Net Rate. The rate provided to wholesalers and tour operators that can be marked up to sell to the customer.

No Show. A customer with a reservation at a restaurant, hotel, etc. who fails to show up and does not cancel.

NTA. National Tour Association, comprised of domestic tour operators.

Occupancies. A percentage indicating the number of bed nights sold (compared to number available) in a hotel, resort, motel or destination.

Occupancy Rate. A tourism business occupancy rate refers to the number of airline seats or the units of hotel room space sold. This demand is usually measured as a percentage of available seats or space occupied for a given period of time. It is calculated by dividing the number of occupied rooms/seats by the total number available for sale during the same period.

Open Bar. unrestricted service of alcoholic beverages at a function. plated food presentation of food on plates by kitchen staff.

Outbound. Outbound tourism is defined as tourism involving residents of a country travelling to another country. Outbound tour operators offer package tours abroad. They either operate the tours themselves, or they commission the services of an inbound operator to handle local arrangements at the destination. The country from which the tourists originate is known as the generating market or country.

Package Tour. A saleable travel product offering an inclusive price with several travel elements that would otherwise be purchased separately. Usually has a predetermined price, length of time and features but can also offer options for separate purchase.

Package. A fixed price salable travel product that makes it easy for a traveler to buy and enjoy a destination or several destinations. Packages offer a mix of elements like transportation, accommodations, restaurants, entertainment, cultural activities, sightseeing and car rental.

Paid Lettings. This refers to room lettings that are paid for by hotel guests

Peaks and Valleys. The high and low end of the travel season. Travel industry marketers plan programs to build consistent year-round business and event out the "peaks and valleys."

Person Trip Visit. Every time a person travels more than 100 miles (round-trip) in a day or stays overnight away from their primary domicile, whether for business or leisure purposes, they make one "person trip visit."

Pow Wow. The largest international travel marketplace held in the United States, sponsored by the Travel Industry Association of America.

Press Trips. Organized trips for travel writers and broadcasters for the purpose of assisting them in developing stories about tourism destinations. Often, journalists travel independently, though with the assistance of a state's office of tourism of a DMO.

Press/Publicity Release. A news article or feature story written by the subject of the story for delivery and potential placement in the media.

Property. A hotel, motel, inn, lodge or other accommodation facility.

Quality. In tourism, the product is often intangible and quality is not apparent until after it is consumed. Quality has been defined as zero defects or defections, but still may be defined by the customer. The International Organisation for Standardisation defines quality as 'the totality of features and characteristics of a product or service that bear on its ability to satisfy stated or implied needs'. Others believe that quality is a combination of outcome and processes, including internal and external conditions, and is obtained when the expectations and needs of customers are met.

Rack Card. The typical tourism brochure sized 4" x 9" and used primarily in tourism racks. Also known as a "teaser."

Rack Rate. The official cost posted by a hotel, attraction or rental car, but not used by tour operators. The rate accommodations quote to the public. Group rates, convention, trade show, meeting and incentive travel rates are negotiated by the hotel and program organizers.

Reach. The percentage of people within a specific target audience reached by an advertising campaign.

Receptive Operator. Specialists in handling arrangements for incoming visitors at a destination including airport transfers, local sightseeing, restaurants, accommodations, etc. Receptive operators can be a travel agent or tour operator.

Repeat Business. Business that continues to return, thereby generating increased profits.

Reservation Systems (Automation Vendors). Computerized systems leased to travel agencies offering airline, hotel, car rental and selected tour availability and bookings. Systems are affiliated with major carriers, including American (Sabre), United (Apollo), Eastern (System One), TWA (PARS), and Delta (DATAS II) and feature flight schedules of the sponsoring and other carriers, plus additional travel products.

Resident. A person living in a given country, whether he is a national or not.

Retail Agent. A travel agent.

Retailer. Another term for travel agents who sell travel products directly to consumers.

Room Block. Several rooms held for a group.

Room. Double: No guarantee of two beds; Double Double: Two double beds (or two queens or kings); Twin: Two twin beds (or two doubles or queens)

Sales Mission. Where suppliers from one DMO travel together to another state of country for the purpose of collectively promoting travel to their area. Sales missions may include educational seminars for travel agents and tour operators.

Sales Seminar. An educational session in which travel agents, tour operators, tour wholesales or other members of the travel trade congregate to receive briefings about tourism destinations.

Shells. A marketing and sales promotional piece that depicts a destination, accommodation or attraction on the cover and provides space for copy to be added at a later date. Usually shells fit a #10 envelope.

Site Inspection. An assessment tour of a destination or facility by a meeting planner, convention or trade show manager, site selection committee, tour operator, wholesaler or incentive travel manager to see if it meets their needs and requirements prior to selecting a specific site for an event. After site selection, a site inspection may be utilized to make arrangements.

Spouse Program. Special activities planned for those who accompany an attendee to a convention, trade show or meeting. Note that programs today are not simply for women, but rather for men and women, spouses and friends. Programs must be creatively designed to interest intelligent and curious audiences.

Station. The preparation, or worktable allocated to dining room staff. It also serves as limited storage for crockery, cutlery and table linen in the restaurant or dining room.

Supplier. Those businesses that provide industry products like accommodations, transportation, car rentals, restaurants and attractions.

Sustainable tourism. This is, according to the World Tourism Organisation, "envisaged as leading to management of all resources in such a way that economic, social and aesthetic needs can be fulfilled with maintaining cultural integrity, essential ecological processes, biological diversity, and life support systems."

Table d'hôte menu. Set menu of two or more courses and maybe one or more choices within each course. The price is pre-set for this style of meal.

Target Audience/Market. A specific demographic, sociographic target at which marketing communications are directed.

Tariff. Rate of fare quoted and published by a travel industry supplier (i.e. hotels, tour operators, etc.) Usually an annual tariff is produced in booklet form for use in sales calls at trade shows.

TIA. Travel Industry Association of America.

TOT. Transient Occupancy Tax.

Tour Operator. Develops, markets and operates group travel programs that provide a complete travel experience for one price and includes transportation (airline, rail, motorcoach, and/or ship), accommodations, sightseeing, selected meals and an escort. Tour operators market directly to the consumer, through travel agents and are beginning to be listed on computerized reservation systems.

Tour Wholesaler. An individual or company that sells tour packages and tour product to travel agents. Tour wholesalers usually receive a 20% discount from accommodations, transportation companies and attractions and pass on a 10 to 15% discount to the retail agent.

Tourism Receipts. Tourism Receipts (TR) measures the total revenue received by Singapore from tourism activity. It includes all payments and prepayments for goods and services made by visitors, transit passengers, air & sea crew and foreign students (staying for one year or less) during their stay in Singapore. Visitors' payments to our national carriers (SIA & Silk Air) for international transport are also included.

Tourism. The business of providing and marketing services and facilities for pleasure travellers. Thus, the concept or tourism is of direct concern to governments, carriers, and the lodging, restaurant and entertainment industries and of indirect concern to virtually every industry and business in the world.

Tourist. Temporary visitor staying at least twenty-four hours in the country visited for a purpose classified as either holiday (recreation, leisure, sport and visit to family, friends or relatives), business, official mission, convention, or health reasons.

Tourist/Visitor/Traveler. Any person who travels either for leisure or business purposes more than 100 miles (round-trip) in a day or who stays overnight away from his/her primary domicile.

Trade Show. A product showcase for a specific industry. Generally it is not open to the public. Differs from a "Consumer Show" in that a trade show targets the professional industry, while a consumer show targets consumers.

Transient Occupancy Tax. TOT or bed tax is a locally set tax on the cost of commercial accommodations and campgrounds.

Travel Agent. (1) An individual who arranges travel for individuals or groups. Travel agents may be generalists or specialists (cruises, adventure travel, conventions and meetings.) The agents receive a 10 to 15% commission from accommodations, transportation companies and attractions for coordinating the booking of travel. They typically coordinate travel for their customers at the same or lower cost than if the customer booked the travel on his/her own. (2) The individual who sells travel services, issues tickets and provides other travel services to the travel services to the traveller sat the retail level.

Travel Product. Refers to any product or service that is bought by or sold to consumers of trade including accommodations, attractions, events, restaurants, transportation, etc.

Travel Seasons. Travel industry business cycles including: *Peak:* Primary travel season *Off Peak:* Period when business is slowest *Shoulder:* Period between peak and off peak periods when business is stronger, but has room for growth.

Travel Trade. The collective term for tour operators, wholesalers and travel agents.

Travel. Leisure and other travel including travel for business, medical care, education, etc. All tourism is travel, but not all travel is tourism.

Traveler. Definitions very, but in general a traveler is someone who leaves their own economic trade area, (usually going a distance of a minimum of fifty to one hundred miles) and stays overnight. Someone who leaves his or her own economic trade area, (usually going a distance of a minimum of fifty to one hundred miles) and stays overnight.

Underdevelopment. Within development theory, the concept of underdevelopment suggests that wealthy capitalist countries have held back the development of so-called Third World countries. Tourism in Third World destinations is controlled for the economic benefit of foreign owners, reinforces dependency, lacks involvement of local decision makers, leads to negative sociocultural impacts, and results in the promotion of staged attractions to capture an international tourism market.

Urban recreation. The concept of urban recreation covers recreational activity that takes place in an urban environment in contrast to a rural setting. Participants in such activities are either urban residents themselves, day visitors from rural areas, or tourists. The major activities are shopping, visits to heritage sites, museums, movie theatres, operas, sport and music events, and indoor sports activities.

VFR. Visiting friends and relatives

Visitor Arrivals. Includes all who go through immigration clearance regardless of length of stay. This excludes the following: (i) All Malaysian citizens arriving by land, (ii) Returning Singapore citizens residing abroad, (iii) Non-resident air and sea crew (except for sea crew flying in to join ship), (d) All visitors arriving and leaving Singapore on the same ship/vessel and stayed in Singapore for less than 24 hours are not required to complete Disembarkation/Embarkation (D/E) cards, if passenger manifest is submitted, (iv) All organised tour groups leaving Singapore for Johor Bahru, Batam and Bintan, returning on the same day are not required to complete Disembarkation/Embarkation (D/E) cards, if passenger manifest is submitted, (v) Air transit passengers

Visitor Expenditure. Includes expenditure incurred during a visitor's stay in Singapore, or prepayment by non-package tour visitors (this took effect from 1995). This excludes: (a) international air and sea fare. It is made up of the following components: (a) Shopping, (b) Accommodation, (c) Entertainment, (d) Sightseeing, (e) Food & beverage (f) Local transportation, (g) Medical/dental treatment, (h) Miscellaneous

Visitor. Any person visiting a country other than that in which he has his usual place of residence for any reason other than following an occupation remunerated from within the country visited.

Visitors Center. Travel information center located at a destination to make it easier for visitors to plan their stay; often operated by a convention and visitors bureau, chamber of commerce or tourism promotion organization.

Vouchers. Forms or coupons provided to a traveler who purchases a tour that indicate that certain tour components have been prepaid. Vouchers are then exchanged for tour components like accommodations, meals, sightseeing, theater tickets, etc. during the actual trip.

World Tourism Organisation. The World Tourism Organisation, a UN-related institution based in Madrid that collects data on tourism and lobbies on behalf of the industry.

World Travel and Tourism Council. The WTTC is made up of chief executives from all sectors of the tourism industry, including accommodation, catering, cruises, entertainment, recreation, transportation and travel-related services.

Bibliography

Armstrong, R.W., Seng, T.B. (2000), "Corporate-customer satisfaction in the banking industry of Singapore", *International Journal of Bank Marketing*, Vol. 18 No.3, pp. 97-111.

Barton, L., Eichelberger, J. (1994), "Sexual harassment: assessing the need for corporate policies in the workplace", *Executive Development*, Vol. 7 No.1, pp. 24-8.

Bell, C., Newby, H. (1976), "Husbands and wives: the dynamics of the deferential dialectic", in Barker, D.L., Allen, S. (Eds),*Dependence and Exploitation in Work and Marriage*, Longman, London

Bennett, R., Krebs, G. (1993), "Chambers of Commerce in Britain and Germany: the Challenges of the Single Market", in Bennett, R.J., Krebs, G., Zimmermann, H. (Eds),*Chambers of Commerce in Britain and Germany and the Single European Market*, Anglo-German Foundation, London, pp. 1-38.

Bian, Y., Ang, S. (1997), "Guanxi networks and job mobility in China and Singapore", *Social Forces*, Vol. 75 No.3, pp. 981-1005.

Burgess, C. (1994), "The education and training needs of the hotel financial controller", *International Journal of Contemporary Hospitality Management*, Vol. 6 No.5, pp. 9-13.

Burgess, C. (1996), "A profile of the hotel financial controller in the United Kingdom, United States and Hong Kong", International Journal of Hospitality Management, Vol. 15 No.1, pp. 19-28.

Burgess, J. (1982), "Perspectives on gift exchange and hospitable behaviour", *International Journal of Hospitality Management*, Vol. 1 No.1, pp. 49-57.

Campbell, M, Baldwin, S (1993), "Recruitment difficulties and skill shortages: an analysis of labour market information in Yorkshire and Humberside", *Regional Studies*, Vol. 27 pp. 271-80.

Campbell, M. (1999), *Learning Pays and Learning Works*, Prolog, Ipswich, NACETT.

Canina, L. (1996), "Underpricing and overperformance: initial public offerings in the hospitality industry", *Cornell Hotel and Restaurant Administration Quarterly*, Vol. 37 No.5, pp. 18-25.

Carper, J (1993), "The painful truth: operations is no longer King", *Hotels*, Vol. 50.

Clifton, W.J., Johnson, K. (1994), "A structural analysis of the European hotel sector: a simple case of déjà-vu?", *International Journal of Contemporary Hospitality Management*, Vol. 6 No.4, pp. vii-viii.

Close, A., Teare, R. (1990), "Effective management development", *International Journal of Contemporary Hospitality Management*, Vol. 2 No.4, pp. i-ii.

CNAA (1992), *CNAA Tourism Degree Review*, CNAA, London.

Collins, G. (1995), "Information technology trends: impact on hotel corporations", *FIU Hospitality Review*, Vol. 13 No.1.

de Souza, A.R, Stutz, F.P (1994), *The World Economy: Resource, Location, Trade, and Development*, Macmillan College Publishing Company, New York, NY.

Deakins, D. (1996), *Entrepreneurs and Small Firms*, McGraw-Hill, London.

Dean, R.A. (1983), "Reality shock: the link between socialisation and organisational commitment", *Journal of Management and Development*, Vol. 2 No.4, pp. 55-65.

Deery, M, Iverson, R (1995), "Enhancing productivity: intervention strategies for employee turnover",

Proceedings of IAHMS Spring Conference, Norwich Hotel School, Norwich.

Dewey, J. (1916), *Democracy and Education*, Macmillan, London.

Dex, S (1991), *Life and Work History Analyses: Qualitative and Quantitative Developments*, Routledge, London.

Ditmer, L., Xiaobo, L. (1996), "Personal politics in the Chinese Danwei under reform", *Asian Survey*, Vol. 36 No.3, pp. 246-67.

Fenich, G.G. (1996), "The uses and abuses of multipliers: a current case", *Hospitality Research Journal*, Vol. 20 No.1, pp. 101-8.

Ferreira, R. (1998), "A comparison of the response rates, return times, return methods and costs for surveys faxed and mailed in clubs", *Journal of Hospitality & Tourism Research*, Vol. 21 No.3, pp. 81-91.

Fockler, S. (1996), "All-suite hotels in the USA", Travel and Tourism Analyst, Vol. 3 pp. 44-64.

Hartline, M.D., Jones, K.C. (1996), "Employee performance cues in a hotel service environment: influence on perceived service quality, value, and word-of-mouth intentions", *Journal of Business Research*, Vol. 35 No.3, pp. 207-15.

Harwood, C., Pieters, G. (1990), "How to Manage Quality Improvement", *Quality Progress*, No.March.

Hasek, G. (1992), "Country lodging seeks perfection", *Hotel & Motel Management*, Vol. 207 No.5, pp. 1.

Hassmiller, B. (2000), "Compensation and benefits survey 2000", *The Bottomline*, Vol. 15 No.7, pp. 6-25.

Hawke, A (1998), "An indigenous worker's guide to the Workplace Relations Act – an alternative view", *Journal Of Industrial Relations*, Vol. 40 No.2, pp. 304-9.

Hay, J (1990), "Managerial competencies or managerial characteristics", *Journal of Management Education and Development*, Vol. 21 No.5, pp. 305-15.

Jarvis, L.P., Mayo, E.J. (1986), "Winning the market-share game", *The Cornell Hotel and Restaurant Administration Quarterly*, pp. 73-9.

Karmarkar, U. (2004), "Will you survive the services revolution?", *Harvard Business Review*, Vol. 82 No.6, pp. 100-8.

Kasavana, M.L. (1992), "Extending the boundaries of hospitality education", Vol. 10 No.1, pp. 65-74.

Katz, S. (1996), "Restructuring for the twenty-first century", in Franham, H., Yarmolinsky, A. (Eds), *Rethinking Liberal Education*, Oxford University Press, New York, NY, pp. 77-90.

Kornhauser, A.W. (1965), *Mental Health of the Industrial Worker*, Wiley, New York, NY.

Kreck, L.A., Rutherford, D.G. "Measuring of foodservice operational success: entrepreneurs vs. executives".

Kriegl, U. (2000), "International hospitality management. identifying important skills and effective training", *Cornell Hotel and Restaurant Administration Quarterly*, Vol. 41 No.2, pp. 64-71.

Krol, C. (1999), "Web becomes crucial to relationship efforts", *Advertising Age*, Vol. 70 No.22, pp. 52.

Kruse, R, Gebhardt, J, Klawonn, F (1994), *Foundations of Fuzzy Systems*, John Wiley & Sons, New York, NY.

Ladki, S. (1994), "Strategies for combating the fear of AIDS in the hospitality industry", *Hospitality & Tourism Educator*, Vol. 6 No.1, pp. 75-7.

Ladkin, A, Riley, M (1996), "Mobility and structure in the career paths of UK hotel general managers: a labour market hybrid of the bureaucratic model?", *Tourism Management*, Vol. 17 No.6, pp. 443-52.

Lago, D., Poffley, J.K. (1993), "The aging population and the hospitality industry in 2010: important trends and probable services", Vol. 17 No.1, pp. 29-26.

Lam, T., Ziao, H. (2000), "Challenges and constraints of hospitality and tourism education in China", *International Journal of Contemporary Hospitality Management*, Vol. 12 No.5, pp. 291-5.

Landry, D. (1996), "Franchise opportunities abound with new and established brands", *FIU Hospitality Review*, Vol. 14.

Langeard, E., Eiglier, P. (1983), "Strategic management of service development", in Berry, L.T., Shostack, G.L., Upah, G.D. (Eds), *Emerging Perspectives on Services Marketing*, American Marketing Association, Chicago, IL, Proceedings Series, pp. 68-72.

Lashley, C. (1994), "Making student learning the centrepiece of hospitality management education", *Innovations in Learning in Education: The International Journal for the Reflective Practitioner*, Vol. 1 No.2, pp. 17-23.

Laudadio, D.M. (1988), "Sexual and gender Harassment: assessing the current climate", *Hospitality Education and Research Journal*, Vol. 2 No.2, pp. 411-15.

Laws, E. (1999), "Two ways of serving pizza – a comparative study of low and high contact services using blueprinting techniques", University of Surrey, Brighton, paper presented at the CHME Research Conference.

Learning and Teaching Support Network (2004), "Accepted students and applicants 1996-2003 in hospitality, leisure, sport and tourism", based on data provided by UCAS. Learning and Teaching Support Network, available at: www.hlst.ltsn.ac.uk/resources/ucas.pdf.

Ledingham, J.A., Bruning, S.D. (1998), "Relationship management in public relations: dimensions of an organization-public relationship", *Public Relations Review*, Vol. 24 No.1, pp. 55-65.

Lee, Y.L., Hing, N. (1995), "Measuring quality in restaurant operations: an application of SERVQUAL instrument", *International Journal of Hospitality Management*, Vol. 14 No.3, pp. 293-310.

Leidner, R. (1993), *Fast Food, Fast Talk*, University of California Press, Berkeley

Lenckus, D. (1993), "A quality solution to improving service", *Business Insurance*, Vol. 27 No.50, pp. 19-20.

Lewis, R.C. (1990), "Advertising your hotel's position", *The Cornell Hotel and Restaurant Quarterly*, Vol. 31 No.2, pp. 84-91.

Lin, M-F. (1997), *Feasibility Planning in Budget Hotel Development*, University of Buckingham, unpublished MSc thesis.

Litteljohn, D. (1990), "Hospitality research: philosophies and progress", in Teare, R., Moutinho, L, Morgan, N. (Eds), *Managing and Marketing Services in the 1990s*, Cassell Education Ltd, , London.

Litvan, L.M. (1996), "Increasing revenue with repeat sales", *Nation's Business*, Vol. 84 pp. 36-8.

Lockwood, A., Jones, P. (1990), "Applying value engineering to rooms management ", *International Journal of Contemporary Hospitality Management*, Vol. 2 No.1, pp. 27-32.

Louviere, J.J., Timmermans, H. (1990), "Stated preference and choice models applied to recreation research: a review", *Leisure Sciences*, Vol. 12 pp. 9-32.

Lucas, R., Laycock, J. (1991), "An interactive personnel function for managing budget hotels", *International Journal of Contemporary Hospitality Management*, Vol. 3 No.3, pp. 33-6.

Lundberg, C.C. (1991), "Productivity enhancement through managing the service encounter", Vol. 14 No.3, pp. 63-72.

MacHatton, M.T., Baltzer, L.E. "Quality personnel selection: using a structured interview guide to improve selection of managers", Vol. 18 No.1994, pp. 77-100.

MacKinnon, C. (1979), "Sexual harassment of working women", *New Haven CT*, Yale University Press.

Makens, J.C., Bowen, J.T. (1996), "Increasing restaurant profits with product merchandising", *Cornell Hotel and Restaurant Administration Quarterly*, Vol. 37 No.1, pp. 72-9.

Margerison, J. (1998)), "Business planning", in Thomas, R. (Eds),*The Management of Small Tourism and Hospitality Firms*, Cassell, London, pp. 101-16.

Marsh, C.J. (1997), Perspective, Key Concepts for Understanding Ccurriculum, Falmer Press, London.

Martin, L.J. (1998), "Integrating ethics into hospitality curriculum", *Journal of Hospitality and Tourism Education*, CHRIE, Washington DC, Vol. 10 No.2, pp. 22-5.

Maylor, H. (1999), *Project Management*, Financial Times Management, London.

McCulloch, J. (1992), "The Youth Hostels Association: precursors and contemporary achievements", *Journal of Tourism Studies*, Vol. 3 No.1, pp. 22-7.

McKenna, S. (1990), "The business ethic in public sector catering", *The Service Industries Journal*, Vol. 10 No.2, pp. 377-98.

Mennel, S., Murcott, A., van Otterloo, A. (1992), *The Sociology of Food: Eating, Diet and Culture*, Sage, London.

Meyer, R.A. (1996), "Waikiki faces major problems: does new master plan hold solutions?", *FIU Hospitality Review*, Vol. 14 No.1, pp. 7-18.

Miller, A., Watts, A.G., Jamieson, I. (1991), *Rethinking Work Experience*, Falmer, for the School of Curriculum Industry Partnership, London.

Mok, C., Armstrong, R.W. (1994), "Perception of Australia as a holiday destination: a case of Hong Kong and Taiwanese tourists", *Australian Journal of Hospitality Management*, Vol. 1 No.2, pp. 25-8.

Moos, R.H. (1994), *Work Environment Scale Manual*, 3rd edition, Consulting Psychologists Press, Palo Alto, CA.

Morcos, S.H., Tak, J., Gregoire, M.B. (1992), "Customer perceptions of drive-thru service", Vol. 10 No.2, pp. 17-24.

Morrison, A. (1996), "Guesthouses and small hotels", in Jones,

P. (Eds),*Introduction to Hospitality Operations*, Cassell,, London, pp. 73-85.

Muhlmann, W.E. (1932), "Hospitality", in Seligman, E.R.A. (Eds), *Encyclopaedia of Social Sciences*, Macmillan, New York, NY.

Mulhern, A. (1993), "The Policies of the European Commission, Small and Medium-sized Enterprises and the Single Market", Small Businesses and Small Business Development Conference, Leicester, No.April.

Muller, C., Campbell, D. (1995), "The attributes and attitudes of multiunit managers in a national quick service restaurant chain", *Hospitality Research Journal*, Vol. 19 No.2, pp. 3-18.

Nailon, P. (1982), "Theory in hospitality management", *International Journal of Hospitality Management*, Vol. 1 No.3, pp. 135-42.

Namasivayam, K., Enz, C.A., Siguaw, J.A. (2000), "How wired are we?", *Cornell Hotel and Restaurant Administration Quarterly*, Vol. 41 No.6, pp. 40-8.

Nassikas, J.A. (1991), " Words of warning, words of encouragement", *Hotels*, No.March, pp. 46-7.

National Liaison Group for Higher Education in Tourism (NLG) (1995), *Towards a Core Curriculum for Tourism: A Discussion Article*, NLG, London.

Nicholls, L., Nystuen, C. (1993), "Future foodservice waste management", Vol. 17 No.1, pp. 231-44.

Nightingale, M. (1985), " The hospitality industry: defining quality for a quality assurance programme – a study in perceptions", *Service Industries Journal*, Vol. 5 No.1, pp. 9-22.

Northern Ireland Tourist Board *Corporate Plan 1992-1995*.

Norusis, M.J. (1992), Chicago, II, SPSS for Windows, Advanced Statistics-Release 5. SPSS Inc.

O'Halloran, R. (1991), "Ethics in business curricula: a Denver University model [abstract]", *1991 Annual CHRIE Conference Proceedings*, pp. 180-90.

O'Mahony, G., McWilliams, A.M., Whitelaw, P.A. (2001), "Why students choose a hospitality degree program", *The Cornell Hotel and Restaurant Administration*, Vol. 42 No.1, pp. 92-6.

O'Rourke, A. (2000), "Continuing professional development: too little ... too much ... too late", the Wisdom Centre, The Wisdom Virtual Conference in Clinical Governance, available at: www.wisdomnet.co.uk.

Oberoi, U., Hales, C. (1990), "Assessing the quality of the conference hotel service product: towards an empirically based model", *Service Industries Journal*, Vol. 10 No.4, pp. 700-2.

OECD (1998), *Human Capital Investment: An International Comparison*, Centre for Educational Research and Innovation, OECD, Paris.

Oh, H., Jeong, M. (1996), "Improving marketers' predictive power of customer satisfaction on expectation-based target market levels", *Hospitality Research Journal*, Vol. 19 No.4, pp. 65-85.

Okeiyi, E., Finley, D., Postel, R.T. (1994), "Food and beverage management competencies: educator, industry and student perspectives", *Hospitality and Tourism Educator*, Vol. 6 No.4, pp. 37-40.

Olsen, M., Murphy, B., Teare, R.E. (1994), "CEO perspectives on scanning the global hotel business environment", International Journal of Contemporary Hospitality Management, Vol. 6 No.4, pp. 3-9.

Olsen, M.D. (1996), "Events shaping the future and their impact on the multinational hotel industry", *Tourism Recreation Research*, Vol. 21 No.2, pp. 7-14.

Olsen, M.D., Connolly, D.J. (2000), "Experience-based travel", *Cornell Hotel and Restaurant Administration Quarterly*, Vol. 41 No.1, pp. 30-40.

OMT (1999), *Tourism Highlights 1999*, Relatório do World Tourism Organization.

Otto, R. (1981), "Occupational stress among high school teachers", Department of Sociology, Australia.

Palmer, A. (1994), "Relationship marketing: back to basics?", *Journal of Marketing Management*, Vol. 10 pp. 571-9.

Pannell Kerr Forster Associates (1993), "Factors influencing the design of hotels", *International Journal of Contemporary Hospitality Management*, Vol. 5 No.2, pp. 17-19.

Parsa, H.G. (1996), "Franchisor-franchisee relationships in quick-service-restaurant systems", *Cornell Hotel and Restaurant Administration Quarterly*, Vol. 37 No.3, pp. 42-9.

Parsons, D. (1992), "Developments in the UK tourism and leisure labour market", in Lindley, R. (Eds),*Women's Employment: Britain in the Single European Market*, Equal Opportunities Commission, HMSO, London

Partlow C.G., Gregoire, M.B. (1993), "Activities of hospitality management program administrators", Vol. 16 No.3, pp. 17-23.

Paulson, D.M., Baltzer, L.E., Cole, R.S. (1990), "Methods of educating cashiers in a restaurant teaching laboratory", Vol. 13 No.2, pp. 31-44.

Pavesic, D.V (1993), "Hospitality education 2005: curricular and programmatic trends",*Hospitality Research Journal*, Vol. 17 No.1, pp. 285-94.

Pavesic, D.V. (1989), "Hospitality education 2005: curricular and programmatic trends", Vol. 13 No.1, pp. 285-88.

Payne, R.L., Hartley, J. (1987), "A test of a model for explaining the affective experience of unemployed men", *Journal of Occupational Psychology* , Vol. 60 pp. 31-47.

Peacock, M. (1993), "A question of size", *International Journal of Contemporary Hospitality Management*, Vol. 5 No.4, pp. 29-32.

Pearce, J.A.I., Robinson, R.B. Jr (2000), "Cultivating Guanxi as a foreign investor strategy", *Business Horizons*, Vol. 43 No.1, pp. 31-8.

Perkins, J., Cummings, P. (1994), "A community economic development survey of part-time labor: implications for the hospitality industry", Vol. 17 No.3, pp. 111-18.

Pfeifer, Y. (1983)), "Small business management", in Cassee, E.H., Reuland, R. (Eds), *The Management of Hospitality*, Pergamon, Oxford, pp. 189-202.

Phatak, A.V. (1992), *International Dimensions of Management.*

Phillips, P.A. (1994), " Welsh hotel: cost-volume-profit analysis and uncertainty", *International Journal of Contemporary Hospitality Management*, Vol. 6 No.3, pp. 31-6 .

Pickering, J., Greenwood, J., Hunt, D. (1971), *The Small Firm in the Hotel and Catering Industry (Committee of Inquiry on Small Firms: Research Report 14)*, HMSO, London.

Pickert, M.J., Miller, J. (1996), "Food production forecasting in six commercial foodservice operations: a pilot study", *Hospitality Research Journal*, Vol. 20 No..2, pp. 137-44.

Pickworth, J.R. (1987), " Minding the Ps and Qs", *The Cornell Hotel and Restaurant Administration Quarterly*, Vol. 28 No.May , pp. 40-7.

Porter, M. E. (1990), *The Competitive Advantage of Nations*, The Free Press, New York, NY.

Powers, T.F. (1992), "The standard world of 2005: a surprise-free scenario", Vol. 16 No.1, pp. 1-22.

Pratt, R., Whitney, D. (1991), "Attentional and interpersonal characteristics of restaurant general managers in comparison with other groups of interest", Vol. 15 No.1, pp. 9-24.

Price, F. (1986), *Right First Time – Using Quality Control for Profit*, Wildwood House.

Prichard, M. (1981), *Guests and Hosts*, Oxford University Press, Oxford.

Prideaux, B., Dunn, A. (1995), "Tourism and crime—how can the tourism industry respond?", *Australian Journal of Hospitality Management*, Vol. 2 No.1, pp. 7-16.

Purcell, K. (1989), "Gender at work", in Gallie, D. (Eds),*Employment in Britain*, Blackwell, Oxford

Pyo, S.S., Mihalik, B.J., Uysal, M. (1989), "Attraction attributes and motivations: a canonical correlation analysis",*Annals of Tourism Research*, Vol. 16 pp. 277-82.

Quality Assurance Agency for Higher Education (1997), *Subject Review Handbook 1998-2000*, QAA.

Rainero, C.J., Chon, K.S. (1990), "Marketing approaches to human resources management in the hospitality industry", Vol. 8 No.1, pp. 32-40.

Ralston, C.E. (1993), "Manager-customer relationship in food service commissary operations", Vol. 11 No.2, pp. 61-72.

Rao, C.P., Kelkar, M.M. (1997), "Relative impact of performance and importance ratings on measurement of service quality", *Journal of Professional Services Marketing*, Vol. 15 No.2, pp. 69-86.

Raymond, M.A., Tanner, J.F. Jr (1994), "Maintaining customer relationships in direct sales: stimulating repeat purchase behavior", *Journal of Personnel Selling and Sales Management*, Vol. 14 No.3, pp. 67-76.

Reardon, K.K., Enis, B. (1990), "Establishing a company-wide customer orientation through persuasive internal marketing",*Management Communication Quarterly*, Vol. 3 No.February, pp. 376-87.

Records, H.A., Glennie, M.F. (1991), "Service management and quality assurance...a systems approach", *Cornell Hotel & Restaurant Administration Quarterly*, Vol. 32 No.1, pp. 26-35.

Reich, A.Z. (1994), "Comprehensive strategic planning as a capstone course in hospitality education", *Hospitality and Tourism Educator*, Vol. 6 No.2, pp. 67-70.

Reichheld, F.F. (1996), *The Loyalty Effect*, Harvard Business School Press, Boston, MA.

Reichheld, F.F., Sasser, W.E. Jr (1990), "Zero defections: quality comes to services", *Harvard Business Review*, Vol. 68 No.5, pp. 105-11.

Reilly, B., DiAngelo, J. (1987), "Entrepreneurial behaviour in large organisations", *SAM Advanced Management Journal*, pp. 24-31.

Reisenger Y., Waryszak, R.Z. (1994), "Assessment of service quality for international tourists in hotels: an exploratory study of Japanese tourists in Australia", *Australian Journal of Hospitality Management*, Vol. 1 No.2, pp. 11-16.

Rejowski, M. (1996), *Turismo e Pesquisa Científica*, Papirus Editora, Sào Paulo.

Remington, J., Escoffier, M. (1996), "Tourism: who needs it?", *FIU Hospitality Review*, Vol. 14 No.1, pp. 19-26.

Riley, M (1990), "The role of age distributions in career path analysis", *Tourism Management*, Vol. 11 No.1, pp. 38-44.

Rimmer, M (1991), "Enterprise awards: are they more flexible?", *Asia Pacific Human Resource Management*, Vol. 29 No.1, pp. 71-81.

Rita, P., Moutinho, L. (1992), "Allocating a promotion budget", *International Journal of Contemporary Hospitality Management*, Vol. 4 No.3, pp. 3-8.

Ritchie, J.R.B. (1993), "Educating the tourism educators: guidelines for policy and programme development", *Teros International*, Vol. 1 No.1.

Ritzer, G. (1993), *The McDoinaldization of Society*, Pine Forge Press, Thousand Oaks, CA.

Roberts, J. (1995), *Human resource Practices in the Hospitality Industry*, Hodder and Stoughton, London.

Robson, D. (1995), "Nettforce and training—the challenge begins", *Australian Journal of Hospitality Management*, Vol. 2 No.1, pp. 49-51.

Roh, Y.S., Andrew, W. (1994), "U.S. hospitality investment in six potential Eastern European markets", Vol. 17 No.3, pp. 41-50.

Roper, A. (1995), "The emergence of hotel consortia as transorganizational forms", *International Journal of*

Contemporary Hospitality Management, Vol. 7 No.1, pp. 4-9.

Rotter, J.B. (1966), " Generalised expectancies for internal versus external control of reinforcement", *Psychological Monographs*, Vol. 80 No.1.

Ruddy, J. (1989), "Career development of hotel managers in Hong Kong", *International Journal of Hospitality Management*, Vol. 8 No.3, pp. 215-25.

Ryan, C. (1995), "Tourism courses: a new concern for new time?", *Tourism Management*, Vol. 16 No.2, pp. 97-100.

Saleh, F., Ryan, C. (1991), "Analysing service quality in the hospitality industry using the SERVQUAL model", *Service Industries Journal*, Vol. 11 No.3, pp. 324-45.

Shah, A., Pell, K., Brooke, P. (2004), "Beyond first destinations. Graduate employment survey", *Active Learning in Higher Education*, Vol. 5 No.1, pp. 9-26.

Shanklin, C. (1993), "Ecology age: implications for the hospitality and tourism industry", Vol. 17 No.1, pp. 219-25.

Shanklin, C., Petrillose, M., Pettay, A. (1991), "Solid waste management practices in selected hotel chains and individual properties", Vol. 15 No.1, pp. 59-74.

Singh, A., Chon, K.S. (1993), "Teleconferencing technology: recent developments and implications for hotel industry", *FIU Hospitality Review*, Vol. 11 No.2, pp. 1-6.

Singh, A., Gu, Z. (1994), "Diversification, financial performance, and stability of foodservice firms", Vol. 18 No.2, pp. 3-18.

Skinner, W. (1974), "The focused factory", *Harvard Business Review*, Vol. 52 No.3, pp. 113-21.

Slack, N. (1983), "Operations management and curriculum design", *Management Education and Development*, Vol. 14 No.1, pp. 19-32.

Slattery, P. (1983), "Social scientific methodology and hospitality management", *International Journal of Hospitality Management*, Vol. 2 No.1, pp. 9-14.

Stevens, B., Fleckenstein, A. (1999), "Comparative ethics: how students and human-resources directors react to real-life situations", Cornell Hotel and Restaurant Administration Quarterly, Vol. 40 No.2, pp. 69-75.

Syer, J. (1986), *Team Spirit: The Elusive Experience*, The Kingswood Press, London, pp. 13-14.

Tas, R.E (1988), "Teaching future managers", *The Cornell Hotel and Restaurant Administration Quarterly*, Vol. 29 No.2, pp. 41-3.

Teixeira, R.M., Fletcher, J., Westlake, J. (2000), "Ensino superior em turismo: experiência do reino unido", *Turismo em Análise*, ECA, Universidade de São Paulo, São Paulo., Vol. 11 No.2.

Telfer, E. (1996), *Food for Thought, Philosophy of Food*, Routledge, London.

Templeton, W., Bond, C.A. (1999), "Banking on the euro· changes and challenges", *Managerial Finance*, Vol. 25 No.11, pp. 17-26.

Tether, M. (1994), *The Legal Challenges of Competitive Tendering - The Problem of TUPE: Employment and Reorganisation Issues*, Financial Times Conferences, London, 7 February, pp. 1-7.

Van Dyke, T., Strick, S. (1990), "Recruitment, selection and retention of managers in the hotel and restaurant industry", FIUHospitalityReview, Vol. 8 No. 1, pp. 1-9.

Van Hoof, H.B., Verbeeten, M.J.,, Combrink, T.E. (1996), "Information technology revisited—international lodging industry technology needs and perceptions: a comparative study", *Cornell Hotel and Restaurant Administration Quarterly*, Vol. 37 No.6, pp. 66-91.

Velasquez, M.G. (1998), Business Ethics, Concepts and Cases, 4th ed., Prentice Hall, Englewood Cliffs, NJ.

Verma, R., Iqbal, Z., Plaschka, G. (2004), "Choice drivers and switching inertia in e-financial services", *California Management Review*, Vol. 46 No.4, pp. 43-68.

Wilks, J., Atherton, T. (1995), "The lifestyle factor: employment practices in the Queensland recreational diving industry", *Australian Journal of Hospitality Management*, Vol. 2 No.1, pp. 23-30.

Wilson, R.H. (1992), "Combining hotel promotions, discount packages, and yield management systems: make sure it's legal", Vol. 15 No.2, pp. 21-30.

Index

O

P

Q

R

S

T

U

W

Y

Z